TEAM

Chardin

Love is the most universal, formidable
and mysterious of cosmic energies.

TEAM

Theory and Practice
of
Team Ministry

by
DODY DONNELLY, C.S.J.

PAULIST PRESS
New York, N.Y./Ramsey, N.J./Toronto

Library of Congress
Catalog Card Number: 77-74584

ISBN: 0-8091-2013-5

Cover Design: John Murello

Published by Paulist Press
Editorial Office: 1865 Broadway, N.Y., N.Y. 10023
Business Office: 545 Island Road, Ramsey, N.J. 07446

Printed and bound in the
United States of America

Contents

PREFACE

This was not an easy book to write, simply because it's hard to press theory, recipes, and dreams under the same covers. Yet, it seemed the kind of a book that might fill the present need for all three in the field of human relations, communication, and community building.

My own team of men and women striving for valid theory and practice went through the hard homework of examining our assumptions, establishing honest relationships, and goal and value-clarification. Out of that experience and our working together for objectives grew this book: a theory book, a how-to-do-it book, and a dream-for-the-future book.

I wish to thank Clarence and Edith Roberts and Rev. George B. York, SJ, whose co-membership on our team has helped so much to motivate and complete this book; Mr. Paul S. Schirm, structural analyst, whose critique helped so much to shape its final form; Mr. Robert Heyer of Paulist Press whose editorial skill shook out so many of its burrs; Lois Thompson, Sheila Fabricant, and Lynne White whose typing was a major contribution; the many w&men who have used it in manuscript form in both my lectures and workshops whose enthusiasm and encouragement urged me to submit it for publication. Finally, and most importantly, I thank God's Spirit for inspiration, courage, and steadfast love to say the good things in it. The not-so-good ones are my own.

Feast of Francis of Assisi
1976

Dody Donnelly, CSJ
Berkeley, California

I. WHY THE TEAM?

> . . . *during the supper, Jesus . . . rose from the meal and took off his cloak. He picked up a towel and tied it around himself. Then he poured water into a basin and began to wash his disciples' feet and dry them with the towel he had around him . . . he said to them: "Do you understand what I just did for you? If I washed your feet —I who am Teacher and Lord—then you must wash each other's feet. What I just did was to give you an example: as I have done, so you must do. . . . Once you know all these things, blest will you be if you put them into practice" (John 13:1-17).*

I suggest the use of TEAM as a vehicle for the sharing of talents in service to church or civic community not to disparage individual service but to emphasize that our present period of rapid social change seems to me to call for such a form. The team has a circular, not a pyramidal structure, to mirror the *shared* responsibility, participation, and decision-making that strongly characterize it. In a circle, no one individual rules as at the apex of the structure.

Why a sharing model, a circle? Because I feel that the needs of people today could be better met by the use of such a vehicle. I believe that a team might better address itself to the psychological, sociological, and theological needs around us.

Perhaps another figure might clarify why these needs are presently affecting us—that of the "See-Level" (CE^4), a combination of one "C" and four "E" 's: Culture, Education, Experience, Environment, and Expectations (see Chart I: Behavior). Out of these we do much of our seeing. For instance, you are reading this text at your own particular "See-Level" (CE^4-Level) or "Way-to-See" produced from the cultures you've lived in, your formal and informal education, all of your experiences, all of your environments, and the expectations ticking in you right now in regard to the future. They might even be making you read this book. Far from determining our responses, this view of See-Level always leaves room for God's action through any one of these five components or in any other way God chooses.

I submit that today socio-cultural change in American life has caused a major land-shift in our See-Levels, and has aggravated our particular needs through fear, confusion, and frustration. Psychologically, sociologically, and theologically, many of us are shaken and uncertain. Three significant consequences follow. First, our value-system has been directly affected by the bombarding of our See-Level with new and often contradictory input. Secondly, our attitudes have been deeply challenged in consequence of the shock to our values. Finally, our behavior shows in practice the results of the challenge to values and attitudes. How do we adjust? How do we handle this flood of input?

For Catholics, this flood of See-Level-input pushing for change occurred in the teaching of Vatican II calling for maturity and responsibility in the formation of one's own conscience. These two values are most necessary for good team serving. That call was translated by some into questioning conformist behaviors. That questioning led to changes in behavior, especially in lifestyles, e.g., ways of receiving the sacraments. For many, it seemed that the former method of "going to confession" was no longer meaningful and they found meaning in communal penance services that stressed responsibility for reconciliation with the community.

In business, too, this same challenge to values and search for meaning appeared in the change of attitude in some young people who moved in their careers from a goal-oriented to a role-oriented work philosophy. Still others, not interested in money as a motivating factor in their lives, discounted both saving and hoarding; rather, they saw money as a tool for finding meaningful activity in art, music, literature, dance, and through religion as well.

Again, the push for personhood we see around us is another facet of value-challenge. People want to be treated justly, to be free to decide their life-style, to be liberated from demeaning and undignified social forms. This need appears in the women's and

CHART I — BEHAVIOR

I. *SOME FACTORS INVOLVED IN BEHAVIOR:*

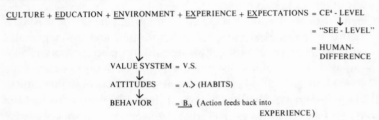

$\underline{C}$ULTURE + $\underline{E}$DUCATION + $\underline{EN}$VIRONMENT + $\underline{EX}$PERIENCE + $\underline{EX}$PECTATIONS = CE^4 - LEVEL

= "SEE - LEVEL"

= HUMAN-
   DIFFERENCE

VALUE SYSTEM = V.S.

ATTITUDES = A.> (HABITS)

BEHAVIOR = $\underline{B.}$, (Action feeds back into
   EXPERIENCE)

DYNAMIC MODEL OF CE^4 (SEE-LEVEL) and its INFLUENCE ON BEHAVIOR:

CE⁴ (See) Level

Behavior   Uniqueness   Value System   { The CYCLE of EXPERIENCE

Habits

Norms   Attitudes

ethnic movements where changed attitudes have produced changed behavior.

As a result of these challenges to values, attitudes, and behavior, I feel that new sociological models are necessary to help supply the needs surfaced by such challenges to develop maturity, responsibility, and personhood. The pyramid (as we shall see in detail below: Section VII) seems no longer capable of serving as the only sociological model or structure that can "grow humans" and serve society's needs. I feel that the team-circle is a viable alternative.

Expanded forms of the team already occur in the communes and communities that band together in search of meaning and support. People seem to feel that like-minded persons can find strength in unity. This trend shows itself on a still larger scale in the establishment of coalitions,[1] particularly of the political variety. These coalitions are groupings of organizations whose members pool resources and structural power to achieve some chosen common goal in a corporate effort. Teams often exist at the heart of such communes, communities, and coalitions, but they constitute a more intensively committed, trained, and mutually accountable grouping (see Section V below).

In a word, I believe we live in an age that grows ever more aware of the *social* dimensions of its responsibilities. "Social sin" has suddenly come into our consciousness, for we are taught day by day that we are not isolated individuals but persons whose every action can affect the ecology, the environment, and even the life-breath of others. Theologically, too, we are learning that we are responsible for the social structures serving us, that we actually own them, for we pay to maintain them: e.g., government, education, and prisons.

But social sin needs social healing: structure to structure. I suggest that the circular model of the team is an excellent training form for such confrontation and healing, since reconciliation of persons and of structures is the basic goal of the team (see Section IV below). The team may be able to help the individual move from an act-centered to an actor-centered viewpoint that takes into account our attitudes and habits, one that implies the freedom of choice and full responsibility of the actor. In the milieu of the team s(he) can, through dialogue, perhaps be able to make more enlightened decisions and face social responsibility through the support of team members and through team structure and method.

The team can also help control our need to attack what we term evil, overcome as we often are by the urgency of human need about us. This means we are calling for a change of heart on the part of some people who are part of the structure we reproach. We are, then, in the business of calling for changes. We are engaged in so small a thing as the transformation of the world. We want to release the Spirit's dynamism within society. Still our goals (what) and the means (how) have to be decided. I see the team as helpful in the observing, judging, and acting that we will need to do. The team circle helps provide a forum for discussing, deciding, and discerning together, which, in turn, can move us from judgment to decision, a vital part of the conversion process for ourselves and others:

Both judgment and decision are concerned with actuality; but *judgment* merely acknowledges an actuality that already exists; while *decision* confers actuality upon a course of action that otherwise is merely possible.[2]

How to reach actuality? How to cross the line when so many of our pet resolutions have died in that crossing? One way suggested by Bernard Lonergan is to enlarge the field of consciousness in order to decide. This forces us as knowers of the good, as users of judgment, to become convinced of the desirability of a course; to make our doing fit our knowing.

The field of consciousness is enlarged by *practical* reflection.[3] We reflect in order to act. A very effective way to do some practical reflecting is on a team, for when it comes to deciding how to serve our neighbor, how to pass from thinking "it would be nice" to deciding how to do it, we need the supporting power of co-strivers to be able to say: "We *will* so act":

Judgment: "Our society should change!"
         "So should we!"

TEAM = PRACTICAL-REFLECTION
         (can push us to)

Decision: "Our society will change!"
         "So will *we*!"

I believe that one reason why Augustine's conversion was so traumatic was that he had no support group, no team to share his goals, and so he had difficulty. Finally, the Spirit had to lift him by the hair and carry him across.

All conversion is surely the result of the empowering action of the Spirit, but I believe that She[4] acts most powerfully and easily in the dynamism of a team where extremes can fuse in mutual receiving and giving. For this mutual acceptance creates capacity for the Spirit. It also provides the supportive atmosphere in which resolutions can be kept, or if broken, can be mended with the glue of acceptance and faith-full love.

Lastly, such a sharing, serving team can help keep us honest in the acting. For the moment we feel the urge to change others, to wipe out evil in a wave of self-righteous power, we are in deep water. Serving is not primarily confrontation, though it may *sometimes* call for direct opposition to what seems wrong. Yet it *always* calls for clear vision: *ways to see* before such opposition. This means questioning ourselves and testing our ideas. The team can provide that dialogue.

> To be in dialogue is not to expose oneself to the charges of another, which is nothing, but *to expose oneself to the overthrow of one's own thoughts* and perhaps to one's own doom. He who has not passed through this test with fear and humility, who has not trembled to find himself constrained to re-question everything, who has not felt his argument modified in some way under the imprint of another's contentions, who has not freely accepted and lived through the possibility of such self-sacrifice, he is not a real partner in the dialogue.[5]

Working with, and on, a team gives us the chance to experience that "fear and trembling." It means we, too, run the risk of change: our own. The dialogue, the communication, the honesty demanded by team sharing can help us avoid self-righteousness.

The drive for personhood mentioned above is helping some of us to grow in awareness of the richness and the depth of the potential found in human *difference*: ethnic difference, sexual difference, etc. The circle of a team with its insistence upon respecting the unique talents of each individual person on the team is a model of the future attitude society will have to adopt in order to make the best use of the variety of human persons desiring to actualize their potential. Uniqueness is beautiful, which means that *difference* is beautiful: of sex, religion, race, attitude, opinion, method—all of these make for richness, for delightful layers of "ambiguity."

Here, again, the concept of the See-Level can help us, for it implies that each of us is absolutely unique in all the world. No one else has our unique See-Level, our unique combination of experiences, environments, cultures, education, and expectations. See-Level means human difference. Human difference means uniqueness. Uniqueness means precious potential for creativity, ideas, attitudes, viewpoints, insights without which a society decays and dies of its own sameness.

A team, in its circle, says that the *sharing* of unique See-Levels is what team is all about: to release through respecting, accepting, and cherishing one another's uniqueness the gifts God sends us, above all, the gift that each one of us *is*. Then out of that acceptance God, through us, can move the world. I believe the team-circle is appropriate for an age that needs to learn to respect human difference and treasure human potential. The time for it is now.

The unity of the human family has always existed, because its members were human beings all equal by virtue of their natural dignity. (Pope John XXIII)

II. WHO IS THE SHARER?

*Now there are varieties of gifts, but the same Spirit; and
there are varieties of service, but the same Lord: . . . to
each is given the same manifestation of the Spirit for the
common good. . . . For just as the body is one and has
many members, and all the members of the body, though
many, are one body, so it is with Christ. . . . For the
body does not consist of one body but of many. . . . If
all were a single organ, where would the body be? As it
is, there are many parts, yet one body. . . . If one
member suffers, all suffer together; if one member is
honored, all rejoice together (1 Corinthians 12).*

Always implied in the why of team is the "who" that we are:
embodied, enspirited unique human beings constantly affected by
changes in our See-Levels. From the first moment of our existence
we have been changing. From that same moment we have also
been dying, and because of this paradoxical state of ours (living
and dying) we are also ever in *need*.

The fulfillment of lesser needs can permit us to strive for
higher ones. When we have bread, air, homes, clothes, cars,
money, care, self-esteem, and status, we take off after self-ac-
tualization needs: for our mind, spirit, emotions to grow. So we
are ever striving to fulfill some need as people-feeders and people-
needers. We live on and in relationship—or we do not live, for our
particularity, our individuality, calls for relatedness and friendship.
Loneliness is indigenous to the country of the mature soul. Never
rid of it here, we alleviate it through relationships and love given
and received.

Because we are alone, we also need others to understand our
own *meaning*: who are we? what are we? and what for? When we
go to the theatre to see *Macbeth*, all we know about him is what

he says, what he does, and what other characters say and do about him. So, too, our own self-concept is built into meaning from our psychological self and bodily image—the whole influenced by all the words, deeds, smiles, and frowns of those who have loved us or refused us love.

We are, then, a changing process in search of the next stage of growth. Gregory of Nyssa saw our entire progress as climbing from one stage to the next in continuous growth: "glory to glory" —with heaven just continuing the infinite growing![6]

Our person is our recent past and we, the product of parents, become our own parent through a series of decisions and acts. Self-transcending, ever-yearning, unpredictable, we are a cry for completion, and our dignity is our incredible destiny: union with God, for we are His children. No role is higher. "When from our exile, God takes us home again, we'll think we're dreaming."

See-Level: Expectations

Lots of talk about "who" but let's ask some questions to dig into our See-Levels and help establish who we are from where we have been in order to see what we cherish. Tell me what you love and I'll tell you who you are. Take a few moments, please, and answer these very frankly. Consult no one but your own heart: (1) How old are you? (2) How old would you like to be? (3) When do you think you're going to die? (4) When do you want to die?

Now, once you've been straight-from-the-shoulder on these four, how about number four? How did you answer it? Many possible answers, of course, but did you let your heart cry: "Never"? Surely a part of you—all of you—wants never to die. The big "E", *Expectations*, was operating strongly in your answer to number four. And which factors in your Experience, Environment, and Expectations fed into your world view so that you answered it the way you did?

On what basis are we able to cry "Never! I never want to die!" For some of us, it is on the basis of the value called faith, our faith-assumption; what we take for granted because we believe Jesus at His word: we will have everlasting life. We will not wholly die, but will be changed. So we believe that we will never really die because of Christ who died that we might never.

It's fascinating to look back at the process by which we answered question number four. We could have found ourselves suppressing what that faith-assumption feeds into the answer, conditioned by the assumptions of a "scientific" society in regard to the "unprovable." That conditioned society is as allergic as were the Athenians, once upon an Areopagus, to the notions of immortality and resurrection.

Then, too, witnessing aloud in words, in conversation, is not what we've been used to in a pluralistic culture that doesn't discuss religion with martinis. Lack of practice in articulating faith can help dry it up in the heart, so when we need to respond spontaneously to a faith-question, we find the superficial answer closer to our lips. Who-we-are are culturally conditioned Christians who need support to practice faith, and need practice at expressing it in words. Team serving helps us with both because it can help change these timid attitudes.

From the See-Level (Chart 1, p. 5) we saw value-system giving rise to *attitudes*: somewhat fixed tendencies to perceive, feel, behave, and act in a characteristic way toward persons, situations, or things. An attitude is an inner condition that predicts how we will act, rapidly blossoming into "habit." It is one of the stubbornest parts of our psychological equipment.

Real changes in the See-Level and value-system have to occur before an attitude says: "Ouch! Message received! I will change." Racial prejudice in the United States is such an attitude needing massive reeducation to change values and uproot the bitter plant itself.

When we respond to a question like "When do you want to die?" our attitude toward ourselves comes through loud and clear. Either we believe that we are to live forever with Christ or we do not. This faith (expressed in their attitudes toward each other and the neighbor) was so loud for the early Christians that the world took notice: "See how they love one another!"

What values, then, were we seeking or protecting in our answer? (A thing has value if it deserves to be wanted.)[7] Two values at least: life and time, super-values for us. The moment our faith-assumption makes Jesus our foremost criterion, our reason for answering "Never" to death, we are freed from the pressure of time. We are free to die, not just condemned to. Above all, we are then free for life, free to live and serve.

Consequently our attitude toward life, time, money, fame, and power can change from hoarding to giving away, even to selling them lightly. We're better able to live in community. Our goods are for sharing and our lives belong to one another. In return we can dance, sing, step lightly, able to go footloose and fancy-free. And we can suffer. People like that can make good team-members. And we *are* people like that, capable of community because through Jesus we have become *new* women and men:

> For if we have been united with him in a death like his we shall certainly be united with him in a resurrection like his. . . . For if we have died with him, we believe that we shall also *live* with him (Rom. 5).

Serving on a team makes us live who we are, liberated sisters and brothers of Jesus. To be freed for living with Him is here and now heaven begun, to be made new by Him now. The pain is that we still remain ourselves—with edges just a bit chipped.

Behavior: (Action, Operation)

Attitudes often spawn *behavior*. On the team we think of the self as operating in unison with others. Here the "chipped-edge" takes off, for sure, because we don't act alone. We're responsible, on a team, to and for others. And when chipped-edges come edge to edge, there will be splinters—even lesions!

In the honeymoon stage of a team, chipped-edges are carefully filed, even filed away. But time heals all wounds, even ours, and gradually some of us reassert our need to be ourselves. We reassert our individuality. We want to be we!

However, serving human need also faces *our* needs and egos and helps things happen so that we *can* see, through team and personal reflection, where our chips are, even to the beams in our own eyes.

Besides the See-Level, the process in Chart Two below (Learning) provides even more information about who we are in serving. We are people who learn from experience reflected upon

CHART TWO

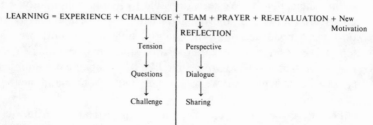

LEARNING

LEARNING = EXPERIENCE + CHALLENGE + TEAM + PRAYER + RE-EVALUATION + New Motivation

                  ↓   REFLECTION

            Tension   Perspective

             ↓   ↓

           Questions   Dialogue

             ↓   ↓

           Challenge   Sharing

WE DO NOT REALLY LEARN FROM EXPERIENCE IN ITSELF.

WE LEARN FROM EXPERIENCE REFLECTED UPON AND INTERIORIZED.

and interiorized, but only if we admit our need for communication: sending and receiving *meaning*. Delightfully enough, our chipped-edges—faults, sins, habits, attitudes that hamper sharing—make it possible for us to communicate, since expressing our disagreements makes for communication; to disagree we must honestly say how we feel. Often that feeling got scratched on someone else's chipped-edge and bounced right back and cut ours.

So in team action we experience our personhood through two great concepts emphasized in Vatican II, the sense of our dignity as human persons and the sense of community. We are community-dwellers in our "global village," the world. So we pursue Paul's "Hold fast to the truth and grow up completely through love to Him who is the head, Christ. Through Him the whole body, solidly joined together by every supporting ligament, grows with the proper functioning *of each single member* and so builds itself up by love" (Eph. 4:15-16). As part of the body, serving together, we can help it grow and we can be helped to know our need to change.

The life-process of the Behavior Circle, the route from See-Level through values, norms, and attitudes on to sharing, is a sign of hope; for in that See-Level, the X-Factor, the unpredictable power of the Holy Spirit, is forever initiating hope and love in our experience of faith-full serving. At any moment, at Her own time, breaking into our experience, She can and does lift us with power and fill us with joy. That breakthrough can be prepared for by our going through the Learning Circle, adding reflection and prayer to experience, on to decision and reevaluating, always a part of what it means to be open to the Spirit. Teilhard points out how painful that openness may be:

To create . . . brings with it an inner torment which prevents those who face its hazards from sinking into the quiet and closed-in life wherein grows the vice of egoism. An honest workman not only surrenders his tranquility and peace once for all, but must learn to abandon over and over again *the form* which his . . . thought first took, and *go* in search of *new forms*. To pause, so as to enjoy or possess results, would be a betrayal of action . . . we must transcend ourselves, tear

away, leaving behind our most cherished beginnings. And on
that road which is not so different from the royal road of the
Cross . . . detachment does not consist only in continually
replacing one object with another . . . each reality attained
and left behind gives us access to the discovery and pursuit of
an ideal of higher spiritual content.[8]

Gregory of Nyssa called that process "glory to glory" in the
fourth century, that life of growing in Christian prayer and service.
The new form Teilhard speaks of, I suggest, might be for us today
that of the *new circle*, the team, ordained and not-ordained people
striving to use their power to serve through team sharing because
of who we are, gifted-people, through whom God manifests power
and love.

The Behavior and the Learning Circles round out the picture
of who we are. We are sharers. Our life-experience and our faith-
experience feed us data. Our co-members Paul, Gregory, and Teilhard pointed us to Jesus who gives us our deepest identity: children
of God, His co-servants. Finally we saw that we are servants whose
serving is made powerful through the power-not-our-own of the
Holy Spirit flowing into and through us all bestowing upon us
faith, hope, and love. A mighty commerce is our God. Our delight
is to be part of the act. And, perhaps, as a team.

*Today something new is happening to the whole structure
of human consciousness. A fresh kind of life is starting
(Pierre Teilhard de Chardin). .*

III. ASSUMPTIONS WE BRING TO SHARED SERVICE

The commonest things of nature have qualities and characteristics which are stupendous. They are a revelation to the persons who study and analyze them. Most people, however, find only strange and unusual things worth wondering about, while they take ordinary things for granted.

Consider human faces, for example. Anyone who takes a moment to think will realize the marvelous fact that human faces are, at the same time, very much alike and yet very different. Among the vast numbers of us on earth, every human face is like every other and there is no difficulty in distinguishing the human species from that of the rest of the animals. At the same time, every human face is unlike every other, and there is no difficulty telling one person from another. We should expect all faces to look alike, since all persons share the same human nature. Variety is the real surprise. . . . (St. Augustine)

To serve is to hope for change. But before change for a team can begin, as we shall see below, we need to understand: (1) the *kind* of team we're part of; (2) our goals and values; and (3) our assumptions.

Why assumptions? Because they are a deeply rooted index to our expectations. They lie beneath what each of us *hopes* for in serving together. And those hopes will tick, tick, tick whether we notice them or not. They will surface in frustration, anger, disappointment, and hurt feelings—"I thought that we would do it *this* way!" But guess what? Nobody asked anybody what anybody expected.

Examining assumptions is a big agenda item for the weekend together the team needs before beginning their work together. "You tell me your dreams; I'll tell you mine"—or we'd better not start! When I *assume* that I know how you feel without checking with you I am in danger of making an:

To avoid growing such a set of long ears, let's dig into some assumptions gathered from men and women, married and single, who have tried to work together in shared service. First, let's look at actual shared-assumptions from people working together (with the emphasis here on the woman-man relationship operating in the team).

In general, men have commented that if women worked with them on a team, they feared less focus by the team on the real issues; they feared power-plays by women, the sometimes higher qualifications of women, and even that women might be more aggressive, organized, purposeful, and vocal than they.

Women, commenting about men, felt that their opinions might not be valued, listened to, or accepted. They saw men as possibly too objective and aggressive, taking all the credit for work together, and too dominating in any situation.

Fascinating to see the likenesses and differences, let alone the fears and expectations operating on both sides. We are, most of us, motivated by such hopes, expectations, and often unconscious fears. In the dialogue of team these assumptions can be talked through and swept out of court.

However, women do have some basis for their fears of not

having equal treatment on a team since men now dominate the field of serving especially in denominations that presently deny ordination to women, but let that be incentive-to-try rather than excuse-for-not-risking team activity. The team in its woman-man relationship is the Church and the human in microcosm. It can and it will work for many, for the Spirit is a blowin' for it in the signs of the times.

Apart from the woman-man relationship operative on the team, there are other assumptions to be examined, most of them based on unsurfaced "taken-for-granteds" about what it means to share and serve. Later on, we will flesh out most of them below by looking at the "What" of ministry (Section IV).

Meanwhile, it seems to me that the following are further traps that need to be trotted out of the closet before we *assume* we're ready to roll as team—or that we're functioning well: First, have we settled among ourselves what each of us thinks it means to serve and share? Then, have we gradually and carefully clarified through dialogue our team goals, resources, particular gifts, and methods? How about bringing into the open power-relationships, emotional trips, and make verbal and explicit our communications system: who does what and reports where to whom?

Some team members assume that everyone feels free to express *feelings*, especially those not so socially acceptable ones like anger, fear, and frustration. In reality, not everyone feels so free and we'll all have to work at it. Again, sometimes all members assume that they do belong on a team and on this team, in particular, without the trying of the gold in the fire that may prove otherwise. Still others feel that after a time we'll not need the weekly staff meeting, the weekends of renewal, or the constant polishing of our communications.

Yet another species of assumption is that stemming from our common See-Level, what the culture, religion, social group, or family background dictates imperceptibly. These lie so deep in mind and heart that they unconsciously influence how we think, judge, feel, and act. They affect us all and need some careful open discussion to expose their roots. For instance, we may assume that only ordained persons have the burden of caring for a religious group, that only clerical persons are responsible for the Church, and that serving is to be done from a position of strength because we are bright, good, super-energetic, and well-trained and so are called to serve.

Still others maintain that what we need is more clerics, sisters, ministers, deacons, brothers to form teams; they seem oblivious of the gifts of the laity who are also the People of God. Some also assume that serving will be done only in a parish or in a parish as it is now constituted, not noticing new forms of serving springing up in every walk of life.

Lastly, there are some quite valid assumptions we need to look at with no "ass-uming" about them at all. They refer to statements in three areas: (1) social or environmental factors; (2) structural or organizational factors; (3) religio-theological factors.

1. The individuals in the team and the team as a group will be intensely interested in growing awareness of and checking on their own milieux: the circles of environment in which they operate. The team at St. Benedict's in Oakland, California[9] calls it "Relation-Building," which would include involvement of the parish with the wider community through:

(a) Community Service
(b) Politics
(c) Senior Citizens
(d) Parish Visiting
(e) Center for Black Catholics
(f) East Oakland Renewal Housing Programs
(g) Counseling and Guidance
(h) St. Vincent de Paul Society; aid to the poor

Their attitude shows an awareness of the parish (in this instance) as a "spiritual, social, economic, racial, political, cultural, and geographic context." The team, no matter where it operates or how, will grow in awareness of the real human needs within its purview, and take that assumption into its operating, into its planning, and into its prayerful remembrance.

2. Secondly, the organizational factor demands that the team develop policy statements about itself. These statements will influence their performance, their concept of their task, their evaluation of their relationships, and, finally, of their operation as a structural group sharing service. These assumptions need spelling out as integral factors for smooth structural operation. More of this below.

3. Finally, a third type of valid assumption the team needs to examine: the religious, theological factors that operate and come

to bear upon our concepts of ourselves and of our team. At first, these statements or agreed concepts seem "taken-for-granted." Soon they become intensely alive as real differences in interpretation occur. Where are we in our theological approach to our serving, as individuals? as team? We need to come together gradually on our agreed areas about God, church, service, roles, tasks, mission. This is not the task of a year.

But the trying will reveal those who should and those who should not be working on that particular team, with this particular group of people, or in this special field. Without regular staff meetings and regular prayer and patience, it is hardly possible that assumptions will be discovered and settled so that peaceful sharing and serving can proceed.

Thus far we've considered some points about the purpose of a team, some reasons for the team operation and its shape, the circle, and finally some assumptions underlying that operation. Now let's get on to what we mean by serving or sharing (Section IV), and what it means to serve as a team (Section V). Finally, in Sections VI and VII we'll discuss the "how" and the possible "where" of team operation.

As you've noticed, our basic operational model for the team and for society's structures is the circle rather than the pyramid, because today a psychology of personality, a sociology of gift-sharing structures, and a theology of gifts calls for that form. This is *my* major assumption. I should like to see groups and some structures take seriously the metamorphosis from:

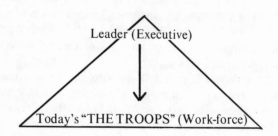

Leader (Executive)

Today's "THE TROOPS" (Work-force)

to:

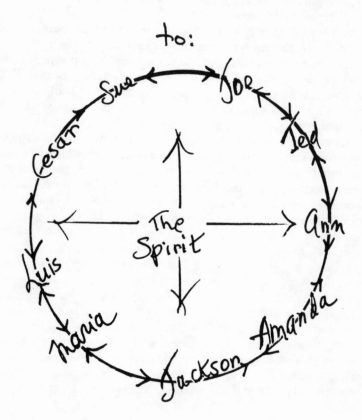

Sue Joe Ted Cesar Ann Luis Amanda Maria Jackson

The Spirit

IV. THE WHAT OF SERVING

*The Lord said: "Say, 'We' "; but I shook my head, hid
my hands tight behind my back, and said stubbornly,
"I."*

*The Lord said: "Say, 'We' "; but I looked upon "them,"
grimy and all awry. Myself in all those twisted shapes?
Ah, No! Distastefully I turned my head away, persisting:
"They!"*

*The Lord said: "Say, 'We' "; and I, at last, richer by a
hoard of years and tears, looked in their eyes and formed
the heavy word that bent my neck and lowed my head:
like a shamed schoolboy then I mumbled low: "We,
Lord" (K. W. Baker).*

What is it to serve? To serve is to hope for change. To serve is
to believe in change. Christians are committed to change of the
deepest kind: *metanoia*, the change of heart we hope for in all our
serving.

To facilitate such change (to share and serve) we need to
remember some basics about the human person, four of them in
fact: (1) people are uniquely *different*; they have different See-
Levels or backgrounds out of which they do their judging, thinking, deciding, and acting; (2) people experience what they experience *privately*; therefore, since they feel what they experience
through their own private-prism of unique See-Level, (3) numbers
one and two imply a need for *sharing* found in social feedback,
since, obviously, we are interdependent for our operation and behavior because we act out of the privacy of unique experience, seeing everything from our own little ivory tower with the two great
windows; (4) *change* is the norm, not the exception, for our serving.

It's important to remember that these basics apply to all of us as servers and to those we're privileged to work with. When we operate as members of a team, however, they must be kept carefully in mind since privacy (1) and uniqueness (2) call for feedback (3) in order that we may change (4) or operate well.

Yet, when we give and receive social feedback (data about how we impress and affect others), we begin to feel the *tension* we saw above in Chart Two (Learning). Recall in that scheme that actual experience can create the tensions found in questioning our operation, our effectiveness, and our attitudes in the heat of using the talents we bring to the team effort.

Perhaps we could say that tension may arise between the way we *are* and the way we *should be* (we think!). That tension is the seedbed of questions, fears, anxieties. The iron is being tried in the fire—all a part of what it means to serve or share energies in the human context that calls out every moment for communication of some kind. And yet so few of us ever receive training or get to practice skills in communication, the life-blood of the team and of the service of others!

In the sharing-situation, however, *our* needs start popping and turn into *individual* goals. We want relief, help, answers, strength, meaning! The tension 'twixt the *is* and the *should be* is the womb of change, of the change of heart—but, we soon learn, of ours as well as of others.

Some of us fear *change*. Yet change, the Fourth Human Basic, is our goal and our business. It's the normal condition of the Paschal Mystery. You and I swim in the flood-tide of rapid social change demanding psychological and spiritual change, both of which are pushed by technological change that leaves our poor psyche limp. Then the cultural bumps we go over while adjusting bring us to the edge of vertigo. Yet not to change (to adapt beneficially to the environment) means to die. To grow—or to die: the choice.

Usually we have some choices when Life says: "Change!" like: (1) kill ourselves; (2) kill the other; (3) stay the same; (4) escape (drugs, drink, drown, etc.); (5) change!

Surgery, psychotherapy, and religious conversion are three possible modes of major change. The Sharing-Team lays claim to involvement with the last of the three: change of heart; Christian conversion; grow or decline.

Conversion is the central experience of the Christian religion, so how does serving relate to it? Being involved in the team and hoping for change in others is our agony and our ecstasy. We are people who want to love and serve our neighbor. Risky business, for we're talking about a human relationship.

This relationship is sometimes called a "helping-one." Depends on how you look at it. Who's helping whom? It's also called the Cure of Souls, pastoral care, or "helping acts done by representative Christian persons, directed toward the healing, sustaining, guiding, and reconciling of persons whose troubles arise in the context of ultimate meanings and concerns."[10]

The authors of that definition have little data on "pastoring by unofficial persons," though they strongly state that "unordained and unofficial persons, non-commissioned, can also bear the authority of the Christian faith to help others." This way, we end up with a "representative" person as one who brings Christian faith and Christian meanings to the help of others.

Philip Murnion calls what we do when we serve in Jesus' name "responding to *God's call* through Christ, and in the Spirit, to give oneself to God and to others."[11] He sees serving as helping people transform their experience of daily life to express and deepen their relationship with God. This responsibility belongs to *all* Christians because they must major in love to follow Christ.

Serving, then, becomes "any role performed to enable others to transform their *secular* experience so that it will more fully reflect the glory of God." That leaves out those who tend to increase the dependence of others or to keep them in subjection. Such do not truly serve. The point is to help other people grow in their *own* power to transform their daily lives into showing forth God's joy, peace, justice, and love. This is the enabling function.

However, Murnion calls serving *religious* when the faith-factor is explicit, taking in all one's beliefs and values because of one's faith. Finally, he sees it as religious *pastoral* serving when it is done for a group of priestly Christians[12] to whom we are responsible in our serving: a congregation, a team, a sharing group, a parish, etc.

Now, this taking on "pastoral-serving-status" comes from the community's saying, "You are ours for this role." Personal call, appointment, election, are various methods of choosing and designating the server. If the community calling a person to serve in their name knows its own responsibility to change life to fit what the Gospel teaches, they are a serving community, ordained or not.

Jesus did·this very thing, sharing His ministry with others, training them with Him through responsibility to proclaim His Father's love. In other words, He gave the gifts of service to His disciples. When He left them, He promised that He would be with them still through the Spirit.

This very sharing of Jesus' serving is what ours means today. Sharing Jesus' serving is "the theological basis for the hierarchical structure of the Church."[13] That sharing is done by ordained and unordained Christians in different ways, so *by what criterion* does who do what?

We're asking about the basis for who plays which role in the Church. Who "bishops," "deacons?" And why don't other people? Again, the idea of power rears its head; this time in another context.

Above, we saw power operating among Christians serving one another. When we mention hierarchical structure suddenly the idea gets impersonal and we tend to think of power imposed by an organization on people and groups under that power.

Yet we saw that such a structure has the "sharing in the serving of Jesus" for its theological basis, so the two differing kinds of power are an illusion. The "institutional" Church is not a biblical or theological concept in itself.

By "church" here we mean people taking Jesus for their Lord whose task is to proclaim and witness to the Gospel by their lives of love and service.

This implies their relationship to Him will be one of true dependence. It implies, too, that they will try to live according to His mind. But to serve others will mean "renouncing coercive violence over others."[14]

This means, too, living in obedience to the Spirit Jesus left us constantly urging us to become like Jesus through serving others in their needs.

This call, when it enables us to minister, is a charism or gift: (1) gift of *sanctification*: to put on the mind of Jesus (live according to His values); (2) gift of *service*: responding to the call of the Spirit to serve the community in a certain way.[15]

We come back to the question: by what criterion does *who* do *what*? The answer is: those to whom the Spirit gives gifts for the community, the fellowship, the *koinonia* (1 Cor. 12:7).

So in the life-process of serving and being served we see ourselves committed to following Jesus, to putting on His mind. We are called to obey the Spirit through the gifts She gives to help serve our neighbors. This serving apparently leaves us with no power over others "unless it were given us from on high," and so it is.

If power is being, our being can cause change, for our attitudes and operative values lead us to behavior, to speech and action. This power to cause change in ourselves is *personal*, but when we can cause it in others, it is a *surplus* power. At its root this power to change others is *influence*. Leadership could be seen as exercising influence in a given situation in a group (team) through communication.

Usually we are tuned to exercising power over others either through violence or imagination. Appropriate change may mean helping people to develop imaginative behavior in a new situation and to forego violence. We want them to continue to be effective and imaginative.

If serving helps interpret the shape and meaning of human experience, to help others deepen their relationship with God, to set them free to use their own power, to *discover* it, then we are committed to liberating others, "not lording it over them." How, when we ourselves are unfree? We, too, fail to follow the mind of Christ. How then can we serve? Must we wait until our hands are clean to reach out to help another?

CHIPPED-EDGE: Condition for Serving

No! The reason *why* we can help to liberate others, to help them discover their gifts, is just *because* each of us has a "chipped-edge." We all have some fault, habit, or attitude just a bit twisted or in need of healing that causes us to rub against others, to hurt and be hurt, and know ourselves, too, to be in need of healing.

Chipped-Edge

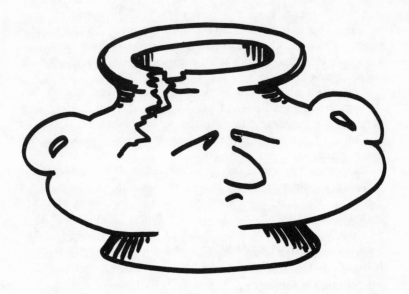

WE HOLD THIS TREASURE IN A COMMON EARTHENWARE JAR
TO SHOW THAT THE SPLENDID POWER OF IT BELONGS TO
GOD AND NOT TO US (2 Cor 4.7)

Serving has to do with receiving, sharing, listening, challenging, prophesying. And that all happens through:

(1) healing (restoring wholeness);

(2) guiding (helping choices);

(3) sustaining (lasting-through and helping-beyond);

(4) reconciling (reestablishing broken relationships).

How is all that possible, especially when it contains such a huge recipe for change? Resistance to change is grounded in *fear*: of risk, of responsibility, and from false assumptions. We get bogged down in apathy, habit, uncertainty about goals, roles, and values, so change seems impossible. Yet we as servant, through presence and mission, call out for change.

When my hands have been wounded, my heart, too, is chipped and humble. Then I do not come to service from a position of power. No, I come with a power-not-my-own to my brother and sister—also chipped. So they can *forgive* me for my service, as Vincent de Paul put it. They can forgive me for making them feel the pain of inferiority that blazes up in even the most destitute when their dignity is affronted by helping that forgets its own faults and suffers from an unconscious superiority complex.

The "chipped-edge," then, turns out to be the servant's *own* need to change. The possession of such a chipped-edge is the guarantee (if we are aware of it in humility) that we can serve with clear eyes, tender hands—and a heart that kneels!

Try it on your own experience. Whom do you allow to help you? Those who don't come to you in superiority; whose words, eyes, and attitudes want only humbly to be with you or to help. Never those who condescend to give you time, money, advice.

We can only well serve another human person if we know the help (the *real* help) is not coming from our power. If we realize they are our brothers and sisters who need help at *this* moment and "our turn is tomorrow." I serve as a privilege, *my* privilege.

Can We Fast?

That leads us to the natural follow-up of such a viewpoint: if we, too, are chipped, if we're coming as privileged to be able to share, if the power for change in the other is the Holy Spirit's, then the *time schedule* for change is the Spirit's too.

Most insidiously, we tend in serving to ask for wages. A salary? No. But much higher wages. We most unconsciously *demand* that the person we serve will change to please us. We never say that. Perhaps we never even face it in prayer, but the temptation is very deep and will surface at the most inconvenient moments! I may feel a keen disappointment that Ted, the teen-ager I work with, is not becoming fervent, prayerful, etc. And I've put so much *time* into working with him!

Ted's clock is set by the Holy Spirit, not by us, of course, and it will go off when the two of them reach the *kairos*, the acceptable time, the day of salvation in their love relationship. How can we clock when another human person should be converted—especially, if it must be on time for our annual report to the school or church?

Fasting would mean that we'd let go the time-line and the big expectations about how and when and where people should change, react, show improvement according to our ideas. Fasting like this might even bring change about "faster!" But, again, that too is up to the Spirit.

Most difficult: can we fast from the very natural desire to be *thanked*? How our hungry hearts long for gratitude! And how often we'll play games to get somebody to express even a shred of it to us. But if we can see ourselves as just sharing what the Spirit gives us—especially if we see ourselves as receiving as we're giving —then the pressure for thanks is off.

The truth is that maybe *we* should be doing the thanking. The reciprocal process of sharing in service feeds our minds and hearts and souls as we serve, so who's the giver or receiver? Finally it's all just a happy blur. But if the Spirit knows we need thanks—or appreciation—it will arrive, and on time!

Stamp Out Perfection! "S.O.P."

What God really doesn't need is *our* perfection so that healing can happen. Our chipped-edge, our need to change, is the river-bed, dry and empty, our yearning capacity for the Holy Spirit to sweep in with power and healing as we turn to others in compassion. Then we can share (2 Cor. 1:5).

Not because we are now strong and good and perfect, but

because our own weakness is a cry for God's strength: "When I'm weak, then I'm strong." Being aware of my own weakness as I serve others lets sharing happen without harm to the served or the servant. Service in Christ through the Spirit can happen only because both of us have chipped-edges, human limitations we can share.

Then as servants we rejoice to say "I'm *not* OK; You're *not* OK, and that's OK . . . because of Jesus. When He died for us on the Cross, he breathed forth the Spirit who makes us OK enough to grow out of despair of ourselves (a definition of 'salvation')." We are freed for sharing with others, true. But, *most importantly*, freed for *receiving* from those we serve: their forgiveness, their gifts, their allowing us to grow through serving them.

Finally, a good-sized chipped-edge frees us for sharing with other men and women searching for community and hope. Together, we let-go and let-God, which permits our self-fulfillment, the achieving of freedom for communion with others.

The chipped-edge is God's way to get to us, to break us open enough so that we can safely approach others in service. The chipped-edge is our way, too, to get to our neighbor who can be reached by the power-not-our-own because we *know* it's not, and our attitude will show it.

We can serve in the space between: the tension 'twixt *is* and *should-be*. Our chipped-edge let's us experience need for others in that tension. So, gradually, feeling that chip, we swing free, free to die to a false idea of what it means to be human, to be Christian—or to serve.

Truly, to serve is to die to a false image of the human and of serving. For the goal of serving is to disappear,[16] to be replaced. With power-not-our-own we serve to make room for others to grow, live, discover *their* gifts; we grow people! Which is what Jesus' life was all about—and so He disappeared.

Now the meaning of serving changes from leadership having to do with influencing others in a given situation through communication to a deeper concept. We now see this "sharing-serving" as exercising influence, yes, but *multiplied by the Spirit's power* in us, in the team or the community, through communication and presence. Thus we are gifted for the given situation.

To serve, then, means first to accept my own need to change and to be converted. Then, to realize that my chipped-edge (need to change) is my passport to serving because it is my capacity to *receive* from the Spirit *Her* power. God wants to be reconciled with us through reconciling love (*agape*) (1 Cor. 13) that motivates *us* to change and to *want* to change while we seek to liberate others from what we feel is their unfreedom.

Which simply means I BELIEVE that I am LOVED— incredibly loved, spontaneously, freely. Not because I'm good or sinless, but because God's love, Energy Herself, the Holy Spirit, enters my emptiness, my weakness (which makes for *capacity*)— with the power of love. We radiate that power and love as we try to serve, for *love creates* value in us. God loves power into us.

If that were not enough, my belief in God's love tells me that Jesus Christ took upon Himself all my chipped-edges as He opened His arms to the nails on the Cross. He knows us and those chipped-edges very well, but even as we gaze into His eyes and know ourselves well judged because He knows *all* of us, we also know ourselves well loved in spite of and because of those edges! For He took upon Himself the burden of our limitations, our edges. He made it OK not to be OK.

Incredibly, He took upon Himself the pain of our inadequacy —and in so doing broke our hearts open. For in the tension between being so well known and so well loved we find the power and the energy for conversion, change-of-heart. We cannot stand to be so loved, we MUST respond and try to become a new creature. We surrender. We discover the motivation for conversion—and for serving: *love.*

And so we become part of that mystery—the greatest joy we can know here on earth—to become a part of the energy of the universe, for love is the most universal, formidable, and mysterious of cosmic energies (Teilhard). So faith is hope believing we are loved: "Behold I make all things new" (Rev. 21).

Now we can serve because we're not alone. We have power to transmit—the power and love of the Holy Spirit living within us through accepting and believing we are loved. That love is for us, but also for the community in which it grows, blossoms, and is multiplied. That love reconciles us with God, neighbor, and self. All we can do with love is believe it—and pass it on.

RESPONDING to a call to RECONCILIATION

"Through him to reconcile to himself all things, whether on earth or in heaven, making *peace* by the blood of his cross" (Col. 1:20).

So: to be a sharer means being involved in Reconciliation: our own and our neighbor's (2 Cor. 5:18).

Finally, being changed (converted), loved (empowered) by God will set us on a "Love Road" as we shall see below (Communication). The source of serving, then, is the Lord who gives us the Spirit. And we serve as reconcilers who help God's love shine in. Our "chips" we work to eradicate, but with patience, not panic, for they are our membership card in the human race. We serve person-to-person, receiving as we give. Even better: from our knees and "fasting." We can relax and let the Spirit flow through the special gift to the world that we are: our unique See-Levels. We are the "only filter of its kind" for bringing gifts to the community.

The joy of this commerce, receiving and giving what is not-our-own in loving abandon from an unlimited rich supply! No wonder our primary occupation becomes praise—and thanks! To share with God's power, as God's beloved, means the receiving and giving of our energies. It means we can then relax and live and love. The results are up to God, and not dependent on our super-performance if we let the love shine in.

With this background of what we mean by serving, let's take a look at what happens when we decide to do that receiving-and-giving called sharing in the context of a team.

> *"The members of the Team are a group in the best clinical sense and it is this fact that makes team ministry the gentle blending of the theology of collegiality and the science of group dynamics" (John Corazzini,* Catholic World, *January 1971).*

RECONCILIATION (2 Cor. 5:18)

↙↘

A. THE ROAD (Human Life)

1. God so loves us that He *wants* to be reconciled with us (Col. 1:20).
2. God's INITIATING LOVE (the Spirit groaning within us: Rom. 8) helps us to discover and embrace our "chipped-edge": our hurting: need for change (conversion): to become a new person.
3. Turning to God, accepting forgiveness, love, and power, we are reconciled and liberated, so want to be reconciled with other w&men.
4. Now empowered, freed from self-concern (liberated) we dare to ask w&men to be reconciled with God, too: to become new with us, to share our joy.
5. To sustain such action, Love fuses us into community: known by the respecting, sharing, and obeying the Spirit's gifts.

B. THE PROCESS (Conversion)

1. Pain from chips: I hurt enough to know I need power-not-my-own.
2. I ACCEPT my need to change.
3. I move toward forgiveness: I ACT.
4. I tell God I need help: repent.
5. I know myself KNOWN (well judged) FORGIVEN (well loved) and *liberated* by Jesus who judges: but HE dies for *my* inadequacy.
6. I accept forgiveness and love: I am RECONCILED, I am made a friend.
7. I become empowered by Love and Gifts.
8. I become *agape*-receiver and conveyor for community.
9. I respond to neighbor's need while I receive gifts through serving: virtuous circle.
10. I am Agent of Reconciliation; I can say in Christ's name: "Make your peace with God" so that together we can help transform the world into the Kingdom of God.

RECONCILIATION (2 Cor. 5:18)

A. THE ROAD (Human Life)   B. THE PROCESS (Conversion)

11. I realize that my uniqueness: (CE^4 Level) is Spirit's channel of gifts and makes ME gift. I revel in POWER AND LOVE AND JUSTICE (GOD) not my own, but mine in unlimited supply.

2 Cor. 5:18: My message is: "God is making friends of everyone through Christ."

OUR HEARTS BURST INTO LILIES!!

V. THE WHAT OF
SERVING AS A TEAM

Men create structures precisely because they wish to rou-
tinize procedural behavior in order that they may concen-
trate on substantive issues. . . . A structureless commu-
nity is as much a contradiction as would be an ocean
without water. The critical question for all human com-
munities is not whether they can survive without institu-
tional structures, <u>but whether they can develop structures
that do not convert themselves from means unto ends</u>
(Andrew Greeley, "Structures of the Church").

A. COMMON PROCESS: From Feeling Need to Serving Need

We have agreed that to serve or be served means to be involved in a common process: the change of heart, from heart of
stone to heart of praise, thanks, and joy. This major change in us,
when it takes place, is hardly the uncomprehending action of a
child. Rather, it is characteristic of women and men who have suf-
fered, who have experienced their human limitations.

In that process of change we came to the point of such pain
with those edges (limitations) that we cried out for help and acknowledged our need to change. We wept, then we acted, then
prophesied[17] (we told God that we wanted to change our habits,
sins, attitudes). We told God that we couldn't go it alone; we needed help.

So we hoped—hoped in His power, mercy, and healing love.
Finally, we were reconciled to God and ourselves: we accepted forgiveness, believed in God's love, felt ourselves being changed.

The psychologist would say we had a new identity. Paul would call us a "new creature," (2 Cor. 5:19) for we have just been through the process called "conversion," one of many such in our lives.

One result of conversion is to thrust us out to involvement with the needs of others. We become gradually more conscious, more aware of their needs through the love of the Spirit working in us.

Soon, that desire to help, that growing awareness, can lead us into serving with others, like-minded and also anxious to serve. This healthy dynamic is born of my accepting my own need to change which makes me safer for serving or calling for change in others. Never on my own account. Only the Spirit can call for change of heart. We don't really know *which* changes are needed in others, so through presence, prayer, love, and acceptance of them as they are, we help the Spirit through to make *Her* demands, so unlike ours! Yet, as we shall see, our gifts for community may some day demand that we, too, ask humbly, prayerfully, and always respectfully, never using force for our interpretation but appealing to the other as equal and responsible free agents.

Before we examine common theology that could underly the operation of a team, we should look at some *presuppositions* that follow from a *faith-stance* supposed in my view of team. When we try to understand what sort of theology would support the sharing that we've described thus far, we need to be quite clear about these points that I take for granted:

1. That serving is best done by those who have received particular gifts from the Spirit for particular kinds of service.
2. That it is up to God as to who receives such gifts and that we wish to be obedient to God as to how, when, and to whom these facilities or powers are given.
3. That such gifts are given for the common good (1 Cor. 12:7).
4. That the laity (so-called) are not conscious, in general, of their call to, or their gifts for, community service because historical development has so narrowed the meaning of serving that we often assign "service" to clergy or to "professional" people alone.

B. COMMON THEOLOGY

Given these presuppositions, then, when we come together to share our energies as a tean, we need to decide upon a common interpretation of what it is we *do* when we serve together. The paragraphs above have spelled out the "what" of service in some detail, but *team* serving adds a new dimension.

However, let's switch back and study the meanings implied in the "presuppositions" that followed from the faith-stance above. First of all, do we—*all* of us on the team—really buy number one: *That serving is best done by those who have received particular gifts from the Spirit for particular kinds of service.*

If so, it won't make any difference if the "gift-receiver" just happens to be a woman, or a married man, or a nonordained person, will it? And the "why" of our not being bothered by this arbitrary choice for the Spirit's gifts lies in number two: *That we wish to be obedient to God as to how, when, to whom gifts are given for the common good.*

It's very important that we, as co-members of the team, do agree on God's freedom and authority for gifting us for service. If we don't, we're in danger of playing God ourselves. Insidiously that leads us to make decisions *for God* instead of listening *to God's word* in our hearts and through others when the Spirit speaks so clearly in their gifts witnessed by us daily.

We could take the entire list of presuppositions as part of the agenda at our first team orientation, where we lay out where our faith and our theology take us when it comes to serving together: women and men, ordained or not.

It seems unreal, but actually number two becomes the blockbuster (and I refer to all our heads) that splits many a team. We *assume* that we do believe it, but if, in the intensity of involvement, gifts seem suddenly dislocated and dynamically moving around the team, panic may set in.

Especially if our See-Levels have convinced us (often unconsciously) that the Spirit should obey *our* notion of what sort of person can heal, reconcile, sustain, guide, and teach. Then what if nonordained persons succeed, for example, in organizing groups for sharing the Scriptures! How do such people qualify in Scripture? It's time here to listen, let the gifts be tested in community, and suspend judgment to follow the Spirit and watch the results.

I am not here advocating anti-intellectualism, but I am trying to explain why a common understanding of *Who* we think is the true source of power is necessary for team collaboration.

Like love, a common theology will take time to learn (and absorb), but the rewards are beyond any price of time and effort. For if we obey the Spirit's gifts in others, we will be liberated to follow our own unique gifts and so discover the basic theory of serving. Those we serve will also teach us what it means *for us* to serve and which of our gifts are efficacious and which sometimes illusory.

What we discover, also, in team serving that is truly representative is that the "laity" have disappeared. It is doubtful whether they should ever have appeared as a distinct entity that rapidly disintegrated into a caste—of untouchables, at that! Once upon a time members of Catholic religious orders were taught to avoid "contamination" from "seculars" (those who led a "worldly" life), thus ignoring the fact that life-style did not mean the absence (or presence) of the gifts nor of holiness itself.

With Vatican II and the Decrees on the Apostolate of the Laity, Catholics were told that they now shared "in their own way" in the mission of the Church. So their formation for service took its "special flavor from the distinctively *secular* quality of the lay state and from its own form of spirituality."

Today that sounds not quite appropriate for the People of God who were strongly included in another document that states: "The People of God believes that it is led by the Spirit of the Lord who fills the earth." The document continues:

Motivated by this faith, it labors to decipher authentic signs of God's presence and purpose in the happenings, needs, and desires in which the People has a part along with other men of our age. For faith throws a new light on everything, manifests God's design for man's total vocation, and thus directs the mind to solutions which are fully human. (Pt.I.11. *Gaudium et Spes*)

Some of "those solutions which are fully human" and fully

enspirited come out of the struggle of today's nonordained People of God striving to read the signs of the Spirit in their own changing lives. Surely the term "laity" makes little sense if we speak of those who have received the manifestations of the power of the Holy Spirit (who seems not to care if they are ordained or not). Ordination is no longer the sole criterion for service if we watch the Spirit breathing where She will.

We now need an emphasis on the dimension of mutual *receiving* and *giving* of talents among all Christians in service so magnified in team ministry. What we are about is the "unfolding of the beauty which the love of God has placed in every person: a celebration of joy." And the Spirit seems to pour out gifts for "unfolding" on women, men, married, single, religious, ordained or not, with abandon and efficacy! And we discover through the team that we cannot tell God how or to whom.

This is not a disparagement in any way of priests or ministers or clergy. It *is* calling for a clearer discernment of gifts. A team can help this process of discerning (recognizing gifts) through the rearview mirrors of social feedback from team members in their dialogue and reflection-sessions.

The theological issue is: Who is to say who gets gifts and what those gifts are? Most importantly, do we further believe that the Spirit has not deserted the People of God and *is* actually flooding us with gifts? They are manifest in the serving done by people everywhere, especially at this time in a remarkable infusion of power. People are ministering (with or without ordination) in every field of service, and many times succeeding, often without extensive training.

Once the team has made up its mind that as a group they *do* accept the principle of God's freedom to act and to choose as God wishes as to who does what, then the primary theological groundwork is laid and we can get on to serving. We now know that's one decision our team won't have to make; we will discern, watch, pray, and follow the indications of the Spirit's particular gifts in our members, and give each other feedback with humility and kindliness—and accept it in the same spirit.

Serving is no longer considered a "job"—and a rugged job at that. Seeing it theologically from the angle of the Spirit's wing suddenly frees us all to obey Her choices, to be infused with Her power, and to go footloose and fancy-free through obedience to the Spirit's giving of gifts, but safe from self-deception through team discernment. Through our energies received and given, we together radiate one message to all people (women and men): "You are loved; make your peace with God by accepting forgiveness, and so be filled with power and joy. This is how we live; we offer it to you."

Just one example of how liberating this theological stance could be is seen in the case of some ordained people today. Historical development of their role has taken a wide spectrum of the practice of many gifts by a community (1 Cor. 12 & 13) and placed the *expectation* of all of them on one functionary, the priest or minister. All the hats, but hardly all the gifts! Why should they be expected to have them all? They were once exercised by an entire community, as we see in the Acts of the Apostles.

No wonder serving, for some, developed into a solo performance: lots of fanfare, but can one perform at that level every day for a lifetime? A theory of the gifts of sanctification and service given for the community as manifestations of the Spirit's power would allow ordained people to discover, through team sharing, their own unique gifts. They would not feel compelled to try to exercise so many others, often a patent impossibility today.

In some religious groups this over-expectation on the part of either the community or the ordained has helped lead to the present decline of the number of ordained. Vatican statistics record some 13,440 cases of priests leaving their ministry between 1964 and 1970, a figure increased through 1971 and 1972, so that we now have a worldwide total in excess of 20,000. Eugene Schallert's figures claim this number already for the United States alone.[18]

Again, the healthy development of sacramental theology (watching the Spirit's direction) may well lead to changes in our idea of what it is to be a priest, minister, or cleric. Given the evolving history of the sacrament of Order, for one, why is it necessary today that everyone who preaches the Gospel or administers the sacraments (the Eucharist), still has to be a *theologian* or *be ordained*? Rahner doesn't believe that the model of the academically educated functionary will continue to be the norm for the actual community servant (priest/minister) of the future. Reasons:

1. The lack of priests will be too great.
2. The importance of charismatic-religious personality will be too esteemed.
3. The option to engage healthy persons already retired from their occupation in new official functions will be too obvious. (*Schriften*, Vol. IX)

There is no reason why leaders will not spontaneously emerge from communities, as did once Augustine and Ambrose, chosen as presbyters for their groups. Among them will be many women, of course, since the Spirit seems not too much impressed by biological structure in the present outpouring of gifts.

At this moment, the word "priest" is perhaps unfortunate because the *role* it represents is an historical accretion of expectations in regard to functions, roles, and gifts.

The suggestion to emphasize "serving" over the use of a word like "priesthood" or "ministry" has an historical basis in the period of the New Testament, one of radical declericalization in the transition from the Old to the New Testament. René Laurentin stresses the likenesses between that period and our own, again, one of a deemphasis on the clerical aspects of serving.[19] This does not mean that ordained persons will not have a role, but rather is concerned with their freedom to follow, as must all Christians, the particular gifts the Spirit has bestowed upon them and not have the expectations of the present role of priest or minister inhibit such obedience to the Spirit.

We know that Jesus Himself was legally a layman. We see Him speaking as one in His own synagogue (Lk. 4.16). He pursued His career as a prophet (Mt. 13.57; 21.11, 46) increasingly separate from the old priesthood and its temple. The Twelve and the servants of the new community were also laypeople, the *episkopoi* and *presbyteroi*, never described as priests in the New Testament.

Two thousand years of Christian history and structural development find us again faced with carefully examining our church and sacramental forms to discover if they serve their purpose: to witness to the Gospel and to discover and obey the Spirit's plan through the gifts in each person. Perhaps the present historical form of the priesthood could be recast in the context of team service which would base the role/function of each person upon the gifts bestowed by the Spirit and found effective by the community that experiences their service; but more of this later.

Meanwhile, the team could provide a way in which priests and ministers could function in service. For team service will not entail their assuming leadership automatically, administering so many projects, designing the liturgies, directing the choirs, teaching cathechists, discerning all the gifts in the faithful. The list seems laughable, perhaps, but just too real an expectation for many clergy sorely tried by it in many parishes today.

When we turn to Jesus' example, we find Him urging prayer, but critical of the temple cult, speaking out for God against some aspects of Jewish priesthood.

> For the whole of creation was the scene of God's activity with man, and obedience to God and his Word were worth more than all sacrifices. In going beyond the Jewish and pagan need for cultic priesthood, he showed his opposition to a fundamental element in pagan civilization. His disciples too formed a "lay" community without any hierarchical structure. The Twelve are not seen in the New Testament as cultic priests, but as missionaries with the task of proclaiming the kingdom (Marinus Houdijk).

Let's Get It Together: The Theology of Sharing

What follows from seeing the Spirit as supreme authority in our group? From seeing each of us as called (1) to *love* like Jesus— "As I have loved you" (Jn. 15:12); and (2) to *live* according to his value-system, "putting on his mind" (Phil. 2:5)?

I believe that (1) we try to find out and then obey what the Spirit decides to give each of us for the team, and (2) we try (though trying to put on Jesus' values) to respond to the Spirit's call to integrity or wholeness of personality (sanctity).

But that "being-called" takes a lifetime of living in a growing process. A community or team is necessary for both recognizing gifts and following them with prudence and love as we saw above.

It means we're first called to respond with a "yes" to the Spirit's call to believe that we are loved (*agape*) and then that faith gets *lived-out* in three decisions that can help make us whole (change of heart):

(1) dependence on God in faith that shows itself in sharing the goods of life with others;
(2) trusting God so that we share this faith unreservedly with others;
(3) deciding to worship and serve God expressed in sharing worship with others—real, if we truly forgive others as Jesus did.[20]

Responding this way to the process of being made whole may possibly demand commitment to a faith-group in order to live out our faith-trust-love and to receive necessary feedback from others as we share ourselves with them. This process of change creates the womb of further change, the nest for the Spirit's rest. The team provides the social form for such a growing of people.

In the nitty-gritty of day-to-day serving on a team, what do these theological goodies spell out? Some big reliefs, to my mind. One we saw above: the "priest/minister" doesn't have to exercise all the gifts new expected of him/her. Secondly, not *all* gifts (individual enabling calls from the Spirit) for serving need to be confirmed publicly by a sacrament or a sign for a sacred reality.

Donald Gelpi, SJ, suggests that the sacrament of Order confirms a call to *apostolate* or assuming responsibility for the growth of the community as a whole.[21] But it hardly assumes that shape today in many local communities. Instead we often have a "cemented" relationship between the idea of "priest" and "sacrament-dispenser." The community's gifts seem inoperative.

Team members might then ask in their discovery of talents, "Do I aspire to dispense sacraments, officiate at Eucharists, or are my gifts other: teaching, healing, reconciling, administering?" This is why I suggest dispensing with the *title* "priest" for a period of time to allow other gifts to surface and the function to be clarified through prayerful *community* (team) discovery of what role and what gift the Spirit wants for that person. Then confer the sacrament of "Order" as public acceptance by a community of the person (man or woman) who proves (through testing *by serving*) to be the coordinator of gifts for the group, and who will officially represent that group in public interchange.

If the See-Level of the individual or team in a particular culture or environment demands that other kinds of serving in the community need to be publicly confirmed by a sacrament (for the sake of those we serve, not first our own), then why not use a sacrament of Affirmation for confirming such gifts? It could then be used at a time in the person's life when real serving in a community has taught her and tested her gifts. Then confirming in the name of the total Church for service would indeed be thrilling and meaningful for herself and for those she serves.

This would also avoid the opposite pole to our present practice in re: priesthood. Instead of many gifts expected of one person through ordination, we'd have a plethora of ordinations to match gifts. If Affirmation could be a sacramental celebration of gifts tested in service, it would become a glorious occasion important to many besides the one affirmed: her family, colleagues, team-members, parishioners and those who have experienced her gifts "affirmed" that day.

Notice that we've been using "gift" in Donald Gelpi's sense of an enabling call from the Spirit of Jesus of *some permanence.*[22] He sees the gifts with an *habitual* character that helps ground the continuity of the Spirit's activity in our lives.

If we take this view, then, some other important consequences follow for team serving or multiple staff. Not only will we accept the fact that *leadership* (inspirations needed to carry on our serving and loving) will move around the group as the Spirit gives insight and gifts. The very role of coordinator (who may be ordained) may also become *not* necessarily a *life-endowment.* The Spirit gives gifts for a time to a group as pastoral need calls for people to do the coordinating. It is then neither disgrace nor abdication to pass graciously on to different serving (or serving in another community in that role) when the Spirit (through group discernment) shows the way.[23]

I think we'd agree that a member may have the gift of speaking out for God as to what she sees or summoning the community to change of attitude. Yet that person need not always function in that role and may well go on to another group to function there or not in the same capacity. Why not the same dynamic of staying open to the Spirit as to the permanence of the other gifts?

Perhaps an answer for present traumas lies back in the Behavior Circle: the historical and theological consequences of what it means to have a See-Level. Certainly, it means we're creatures of *habit*, and so, involved in the paradoxical situation of worshipping ourselves every now and then even as "church" if we don't catch ourselves at it—or have a group around to help us see our idol-building.

I simply mean that we tend to make habitual whatever becomes *established*, or has been around a year or more: "We *always* do it that way" (the team is only one year old!) said for the benefit of a new member who dares to suggest another method of liturgy, teaching, preaching, or running the meeting. As we calcify our bones, we atrophy our heads, too—and our hearts are never far behind!

Is our first commitment to obey and love the Spirit's direction of our lives? If it is, we'll fight this tendency to worship our home-made idols. We'll not see "priesthood" as an object of worship, nor serving, nor teaching, nor any other role, but will strive simply to follow what the Spirit calls us to through prayer each day. This, too, is basic to a theology of sharing.

Tomorrow our call may change—and that will be good, for we are incredibly loved, and so may go pilgrim-free on after the Spirit's call, not clinging to our little idols; no, not even our team functions. They are means, not end; the basket, not the food. We will trust God—who is with us all days, who is magnificently faithful and eminently trustworthy—a very good track record so far!

Let's see now what a common sociology can do for us as team.

C. COMMON SOCIOLOGY: "It's a *Group*!"

What sort of beast is a team? It's a sociological entity, a group. So it has a life of its own:

(1) It is made up of individuals *accountable* to one another, striving for goals held in common.

(2) It assumes a division of *responsibility* and *power.*
(3) It has a built-in *communications* apparatus.

These apply to many groups, of course, but are absolutely essential for a team. They can all too easily be forgotten and thus cause the major bumps of the formative period of a team. Once we admit that this team is a *group*, we must then admit the need for understanding the nature of the beast: *group dynamics.*

Everything any science can give us we take. What psychology told us about our attitudes is supplemented by what sociology says about our group life—both of them the bedrock for the doing of our common theology and practice: using our gifts to serve.

So it becomes a real "must" that the team members set aside that weekend or week together for orientation. Part of that agenda should be some training in group dynamics. Not games, but real awareness-building about what sort of sociological instrument this team actually is. Have we got us a Rolls Royce or a Pinto, and why or why not? Learning how the engine works is part of our job as a team: How do groups function? What are the inner forces operative whether we recognize them or not?

Goals

Since a pastoral team is a group of people doing together what one person once tried to do, we start out on the right foot: we make sure of a common *goal.* A group with a goal like "the kingdom of God upon earth" has a "fuzzy by the tail."[24] It describes an abstraction, a statement of purpose. The only way to get a handle on it will be to break it down into some attainable, perceptible *actions* that arrive at it step by step. *Objectives* these are called—attainable, immediate actions or performance targets.

Don't hesitate as a team to spend some time taking this quite seriously. Each one could write down the most important goal of the team in silence. Then share—and watch the Expectations fly! (Watch See-Level operating.) Gradually evaluating, sharing what each member thinks we're about, grows our knowledge of each other and does two jobs at once: knowing each other; knowing our own goals and expectations.

Notice that each goal expressed is born from some perceived

need—perhaps in ourselves, perhaps in the community we propose to serve. Which turns us toward a formula that goes like this:

NEED> *GOAL*> *ROLE* (Gift-Discernment) = *STRATEGY* + *TACTICS*
$$(\text{PLAN}) \qquad (\text{OBJECTIVES})$$
Steps in Plan

The need we experience in ourselves to serve (and to serve together) must be in line with the *actual needs* ticking in the people we intend to share with in community and the people, above all, we intend to serve. No "laying-of-trips" from above on a local community that may have no such needs. Above all, we will *ask them* about their needs.

Here the canvassing of the neighborhood, the visiting, inviting into the group, respectfully listening, asking for advice of those we intend to serve is absolutely essential. We as servants do not want to feed people indigestible food. Neither milk nor meat but sawdust because we did not consult *their* needs.

So *need* becomes *goal* (once we agree on it). Meanwhile our mutual sharing, our weekend together, our prayer together, our individual and communal discernment is teaching us *who* has *what gift* for the team. Time and the actual serving of people will prove those gifts. Meanwhile, we fit each member's individual strength to the *tactics* to implement goals. GOAL becomes individual ROLE through discerning each GIFT.

Again, note how this procedure assumes much *time*: time with the local community, time with each other, time praying for light, for strength, time for reading and studying. The better-adjusted, the better-informed the team is, the fewer painful switches will have to be made in the midst of ministry itself. Preparation will not insure infallible performance, but it will certainly help everybody feel better before kicking-off the project and in the event!

Some very real problems about setting goals and objectives usually surface:

(1) lack of clarity about goals (why writing and posting them is *not* superfluous—also periodically reviewing them as a team refresher);

(2) integrating individual and group goals (a real hornet's nest, but helped immensely if all cards have got onto the table in team-prep's weekend);

(3) making sure that consensus has really been reached (permissive atmosphere essential for this).

Nobody really buys goals and objectives they have not helped to set—and set in their hearts to work for. How did you arrive at your team goals? Did one person decide? Was it a group decision? If not, way out there on the firing line it will be easy to let them slip if they haven't been chosen by the group with free discussion, feelings flying, and real group agreement about where we want to go and how in this serving venture.

STRUCTURE = AN ESTABLISHED PATTERN OR SET OF RELATIONSHIPS

That question of decision-making leads us to another vital "what" of the team. Since it's a group, that group has a *structure*, for where two or three are gathered together there will be structure. We have to learn the lesson of the communes: if everybody takes care of it, nobody will—if work is involved. And finally, somebody suggests that we set up a rule or two! Structure is born, but *we* decide *which* kind.

Our society is going through "structura-phobia": we dislike 'em—and often because we've been burned. It's just part of the anti-authority stage we're passing through in revulsion from over-authoritarian structures: home, government, church, marriage—each social unit feels the cultural pressure.

However, a team that neglects to understand and use its own structure can hardly survive. "Know thyself" is our maxim, which means "us" individually and "us" as a sociological entity: a group structured into a team. A team is made up of individuals who have their own agendas and the team agenda as well. So when it comes time to make a decision, how does the power structure operate?

Power: simply stated, who has the power? If our theology of the gifts has taken root, we agreed that the Holy Spirit is THE BIG WHEEL that sets our team wheels in motion. That power is our life, joy, and hope. And the Spirit (well-grounded in group-life through long practice in the Trinity) seems to move from person to person in the team process with insights, contributions, ideas, and emotional strengths.

Leadership training says: "Leadership moves around the group." We buy that, watching and listening for the brush of the Spirit's wing in the contributions of our fellow-members and our own. So we say: "The Spirit moves around the team."

Poetic, maybe, but still precise! If we don't really buy this basic principle—the Holy Spirit is THE power in our structure funneling power and insight to individuals FOR the team—we may have big troubles with the dynamite of personal ambition and powerful personalities.

The model is the same: the WHEEL—the circle of the Spirit's dynamic infusion of power in and through the team, which means the team has to learn to discern, as we saw above. Not by magic formulae, but by that patient listening to each other which is listening to the Spirit and our spirits. Prayer before each meeting (and during it) is vital for such an approach. Prayer, too, is a way to know, to decide, to be taught by the Spirit, to remove personal barriers, and to cement the team through love.

This giving of ideas, listening supportively, building on other's contributions, is the art of team government at a very high level. It presupposes individual and communal prayer, open communication, absence of fear and intolerance. Most of all it can happen only if no one tries to take over the Spirit's function and run the show. Yet, each must feel free to express insights and feelings.

Our SEE-LEVEL has too often taught us that the ordained or the professionally trained person in the group is automatically the leader and the decision-maker. Now, when we try to serve together in the circular model, different assumptions operate: *No one* is necessarily the sole decision-maker. The *team* decides as the Spirit guides.

The team holds the *power* to decide about everything, but of course, an intelligent decision of the team begins to farm out pieces of power: roles, functions, etc., according to tested gifts. But the basic must remain: the team decides. *How* it decides is what it also figures out through frank discussion, expression of feelings, and prayer.

Structures, though they cannot be seen, still do run the show. This practically makes them unassailable, and we can't seem to fight with them because they're invisible—simply because they *are* a pattern of relationships! And yet, in their name, human persons live or die, blossom or stagnate, in an institution or on a team, so vigilance is always needed to insure *shared* decision-making and power.

Once the team, through orientation, prayer, and shared study and experience, makes sure it knows and understands its *own* structure, it has become more aware of its sociology. It knows what forces are operating and through continued work in group dynamics learns to *name* these forces. Sometimes, perhaps, we'll have to name a threat to the dynamic of the Spirit's power freely passing from person to person—and being listened to—for perhaps the circle is beginning to grow a pyramid. Perhaps sharing is weak and an evaluation session can analyze the weakness after prayer and through prayer.

Members who can't take part in such openness and expression of feeling (especially anger or resentment) may not desire to take part in the team variety of serving. Theirs may be a call to a more individual ministry, and team discernment and honesty can help them decide.

We, as team, are a structure. As people serving people in Christ's name, we ask for change: our own and others'. Then, as structure to structure, we are engaged in asking for change from the structures (sets of relationship) in our society as well. For all of us in civilized society are somehow part of a structure: government, industry, university—you name it, you're in one!

If our own social structure, the team, is not striving to be a living witness to the values of shared decision-making, accountability, collegiality, subsidiarity, respect, humility, and love in our own operation, then we can hardly ask society to shape up to please us. So we strive for a valid sociology to help express our theology of sharing.

D. COMMON EXPERIENCE: Measuring Rods for Membership

For the team to work well together some *shared elements* help measure the growing we hope for; they help us experience what a real team might be, and we experience them together:

1. *SHARED SENSE OF BELONGING:* We might ask to test for these:

   Do members feel they belong to the group?

   Do they feel really respected, welcome?

   Are they really part of the planning, the work, the deciding, the responsibility?

   Are their ideas listened to, accepted?

   Are they taken seriously, especially if they are women?

   Do members feel that belonging to this team is so satisfying that it really makes it worth the effort to belong?

2. *SHARED ACHIEVEMENT*

   Is the team aware that, to function at their best, belonging, respect for differences, expression of feeling, open decision-making—all shared in co-responsibility—are essential for successful working-together?

   Can members see their individual achievement contributing to the mosaic of the team's work, so to the TEAMWORK?

   Gradually, can "success" fade as a goal or criterion for valuing one another and "serving-and-loving" become *achievement* for this team?

3. *SEE-LEVEL AS BASIS OF HUMAN DIFFERENCE*

   Do members reflect long and hard before they see another's reaction as dislike or aversion?

   Rather, can they gain perspective through interpreting most reactions as coming from the other's Culture, Education, Experience, Environmental pressures, disappointed Expectations? (See-Level got stomped on?)

   Can each develop the habit of fostering the others' See-Levels with their unique gifts, skills, experiences—making for team-richness and the Spirit's power released?

Do members deepen their acceptance of their *own* See-Levels as producing their attitudes and sometimes unaccountable behavior? It's better than counting 10!

4. *SHARED ACCOUNTABILITY*

How much real responsibility do members feel to the team life and work?

What mechanisms keep them honest by sharing of "goofs" and "glows"?

Has the team designed a way to let people get these both out on the carpet?

Can they share them in prayer as well, keeping our "trying-to-be-honest" in full view of the Spirit's power to help us be?

Who is accountable to whom, and do they both know and accept that?

5. *SHARED IDEAS, INSIGHTS, AND FEELINGS*

Can the team express to each other through their structure as well as informally what they think, their learning from experiences, their deepest feelings: disappointment, despair, frustration, joy, exultation?

How to work out ways so that these feelings can be channeled, not discouraged, evoked rather than suppressed?

What provision is there in the weekly staff meeting for such expression?

How much do the members know about communications skills, methods, training?

6. *SHARED THEOLOGICAL REFLECTION AND PRAYER*

Can the team take time periodically for serious study, discussing (with a resource person, perhaps) the *theory* of the kind of serving they're trying to do?

How does the team facilitate such digging into practice to find its basis in the teaching of Jesus?

Most importantly, will the team set up special periods for communal prayer, not satisfied with individual prayer, though building on it?

Can responsibility for such prayer move around the group respecting the contributions of each?

Does the team see prayer as a help in making decisions, another way to "work through" a problem, an idea, a decision? Not only thinking it through, but laying themselves open to the Spirit's teaching them in prayer and listening?

All of the above aspects of shared operation are directly related to the integrating factor most necessary for a team: a *communications system* and awareness of the *need* for communication. Before discussing it, however, we need to look at our present social and historical situation in which we call for such open, trusting communication.

E. COMMON SITUATION IN HISTORY: The Challenge Contained in Shared Service in Our Society

So far we've seen that shared service will call for a *mutual understanding* of our: (1) common process (from feeling need to serving need); (2) common theory of service (God decides who has which talents for the team); (3) common sociology (what we need to become *a group* of individuals who can form a team). Finally, in the listing of requirements for true sharing, we saw that *communication* would be the key factor for producing the process, theology, and sociology needed to attain our common *understanding* of what it means to be a team.

All very well, but understanding and communication presuppose *communicators*. In becoming aware of how much our individual See-Levels influence our attitudes and behavior, we may well have reflected upon the power of the dominant culture (the big "C") of our society to form these unique values and attitudes. And that culture reflects some alienating, divisive elements that cannot help but affect us as we strive to form the community-in-small that is the team.

First of all, so many of us have a poor self-concept. Somehow we feel that we have no valuable contributions, no good ideas, and, of course, no influence. So much of this may stem from the fact that we may not have allowed the fact that God really loves us to sink in; we may not realize that we are loved, and so our attitude toward self is negative. We don't value the fact that God values us.

Now since our self-concept is one of the most important components of our behavior, we have trouble acting, operating, or functioning in a confident, open, joyful way. Even the most educated, competent, successful women and men in a group are still intimidated by the message of the culture: "people" are not important; YOU are not important, when all the time God is saying, "You are so important that I have moved heaven to earth to prove that I love you; I sent you my Son" (Jn. 3:16).

Another reason for our dis-esteem: we lack LIVE ROLE MODELS, men and women both, of what real leadership looks like. There are too few of them around. Yet, thanks to the Spirit's moving in our time, people are beginning to look up and discover their gifts, to listen to their deep insights, to the touches of the Spirit urging and guiding them into life-roles.

To some people, that urge may move them toward service in a religious body, and for them ordination is a goal. Others are not so sure. They want to serve in society, and that means obeying their gifts and testing them in a real-live community to help discern their validity. Often a team can be the primary group to do this job, while serving itself will separate the gifts from the dreams.

All of us on the team will need to be more aware of our somewhat wilted self-concepts, no matter how thick the masks we sometimes wear. Some telltale signs are: fear of speaking up, of taking a stand, of making a decision, of trusting the gifts we possess, and especially of expressing our real feelings: fear, frustration, and anger as well as joy and satisfaction. As team-members we need to take one another seriously as fellow humans who are people-feeders, yes, but also people-needers.

Both men and women will have to become more aware of our mutual damage from thousands of years of relating resulting in our present painful situation. This includes mythologies about our sexuality, our mutual misuse of power, and our games-playing. We'll need to help one another surface and develop our mutual longing to be equal, free, and lovingly ourselves. Most important-

ly, we will have to learn to believe in *our own experience* as enspirited, embodied human persons who happen to be male and female. Sharing in love and trust that unique experience can give us
a new idea of what it means to be human[26] as men and women
viewing one another as fellow-seekers for meaning and fellow-
sharers in God's love. For us, *every* human relationship can be
challenge, hope, and responsibility: "I came that they may have
life and have it in abundance" (Jn. 10:10).

Some writers have suggested that the model or the type of
relationship for men and women in the future should be *partnership*. Letty Russell sees it this way:

> Those who have experienced the gift of partnership (men/
> women; women/women; men/men; mixed groups) in any deep
> and profound way know that in each such relationship the
> gifts of the Spirit means that the whole becomes an overplus
> of the sum of the parts. This has happened to me in many
> relationships, and I certainly experience it in my own mar-
> riage. I became more than myself because of my husband and
> he became more than himself because of me. We were at least
> three or more as we rejoiced in the gifts each brought to the
> service of Christ in the New Age.[27]

Paul Jewett sees the woman-man relationship as partnership
also—accepting each other "as equals whose difference is mutually
complementary in all spheres of life and human endeavour."[28]

Somehow, I feel that Jesus wanted even *more than that* for us
as women and men. Partnership is not enough for sharers. We
have been calling ourselves *servants* as people who try to share
with others in mutually receiving and giving of talents and energies
in response to human need. Yet I'd like to come closer still to
Jesus' description of who we are when we say "yes" to becoming
His, to becoming part of His serving team. He insists that when we
do that we are no longer servants (slaves) but *friends*, *His* friends:
"I have called you friends, my friends" (Jn. 15:15).

If men and women are to work together across lines of race,
religion, sex, See-Level difference, they can do no better than take
this prescription of Jesus for the goal: to try to become friends.

Friendship presupposes an equality before God based on the acceptance of delightful difference (His idea) which can make for interest, acceptance, joy, pain, and ultimately love. And here's where the Spirit's gift of *agape* (love) to those who accept Jesus' values helps us *achieve friendship*, making minds and hearts one as we try to share. This kind of love grows, endures, and makes us one as the Father and Jesus are one, as Jesus begged His Father we would be: one with Him (Jn. 17).

What can produce such a blossoming? An atmosphere of openness to the Spirit speaking in each person. Respecting, accepting, listening to the other as messenger to me, with a piece of my good news! The power structure of a team must ensure that such give-and-take is possible.

Sometimes this insistence upon the expanded involvement of women in ministry seems bizarre. Yet it is quite possible that ministry may be an overwhelmingly *female* profession in the future. Seminary enrollment and ordination statistics for men show a drop in membership in the field of ministry that mirrors role changes and expectations.

Seminaries are hurting for male enrollment, but women students are knocking hard at the gates—and being graduated, having completed all requirements for ordination whether the culture of their individual church can abide a female presence behind the altar or not. Many churches are getting mighty used to it.

On the other hand, if nursing, social work, and teaching have been almost totally female preserves in the past, that scene is changing. Men are entering these fields, while women are entering seminaries in large numbers. The Graduate Theological Union in Berkeley (nine colleges in the complex), an interdenominational group with international dimensions, shows a female enrollment for 1975 of 25 per cent in its master's and doctoral programs.

We are in the midst of major paradigm and role change seen in women and men's moving into each other's traditional fields. Women may move into new fields *not* to move men out. That's not their business. Men are moving *themselves* out, trying to follow *their* consciences, looking for other ways to serve their society. Although women have seldom functioned in recognized, prestigious, official roles in the sacred citadel, the Spirit seems to be moving them into serving with the experience and the attitudes that I hope will make for *shared* service. Women will welcome men as co-sharers, friends, in serving, and men can relax and enjoy not having to play all the roles for the community.

The present revolution in roles and life-styles will call for a "Pauline" form of service: part-time "official" service. Working only three or four days per week will mean that we can serve as our choice of vocation on the "other days" and support ourselves a part of the week. Why not, if "sharing" means enabling others to use *their* gifts. Even the time we need for ministry is cut down, and we soon are co-serving with people whose gifts begin to blossom. "Tent-making," again, will be our thing.

This common theology of sharing of gifts and acceptance of our uniqueness and difference as women and men makes lack of financial resources, buildings, and funds much less threatening. A ground-shift in the culture will probably change the concept and the expectations of what it means to serve. We will see people paid to do certain special tasks for the community. Others, ordained (but probably not) may well be the volunteer persons whose call is discerned by their group. Married clergy could easily be a part of this development.

Dr. Letty M. Russell in a speech to the National Consultation of Ordained Women in the United Methodist Church (1975) predicted:

Theological education will begin to follow a variety of models which will liberate students to gain the theological knowledge needed by the church, while at the same time providing opportunity for exploring *another professional skill.*

This would also liberate "theology" to become the leaven in the dough of society in all the arts and sciences, a role that would revitalize it and give it a new perspective: a world's-eye view.

If such predictions prove true, or partly so, *team serving—* men working with women in equality, sharing, and love—may become a useful model for those planning to serve today simply because the team allows members, whether female or male, to use their gifts and respect and receive the gifts of others in an atmosphere of trust and love.

F. COMMON MOTIVATION: "Love" (*Agape*)
Moves Us Into Action

It's all very well to see the team as furnishing a vehicle for mutual sharing and serving by women and men in an attitude of trust and love. But we need to *ask* for that gift of trusting love and believe we will receive it. For God is already anxious to give it to us: "So I say to you, Ask and it will be given to you. What father among you would hand his son a stone when he asked for bread? . . . If you, then, who are stingy, know how to give your children what is good, how much more will the heavenly Father give the Holy Spirit to those who ask him!" (Lk. 11:9-13).

We ask for the love we need to share and serve as a team. And then we translate that plea and desire into the area WE can somewhat control: our daily actions, how we treat one another. This process of asking for love (power) and practicing it in sharing is at the heart of what it means to be team.

Let's say that we take the High Road (the Love Road) and the Low Road (the Love Means), one to describe the process of developing a *loving attitude*, and the other (Means) for the steps (or objective) that can get us to that goal. (See Chart, p. 60 below). What we're trying to do is move from a low-level to a high-level of acceptance of the other, in spite of chipped-edges, both theirs and ours.

Note that the column at the left describes the road from superficial to full acceptance; the column at the right, the Means to go down that sometimes-lonesome-road. With the Spirit empowering us, however, that road can become the great highway to the change of heart that *accepts* God's love (*agape*), and passes it on in service in a Virtuous Circle, a graphic of our:

(1) *human* relationships as feeding us power and love to serve;
(2) the *Spirit's* manifestations empowering us in and through those relationships.

THE LOVE ROAD

ACCEPTANCE: This just means I let you *be* in my presence. Not playing God and demanding that you be in *my* image and likeness. I let you be *different* from me. Sounds simple, but need I

THE LOVE ROAD   THE LOVE MEANS

ROAD: ←— LOVE —→ MEANS:

ACCEPTANCE   RESPECT

↓   ↓

LISTENING   ENCOURAGEMENT

↓   ↓

AWARENESS   ACKNOWLEDGMENT

↓   ↓

UNDERSTANDING   PRAISE

↓   ↓

COMMUNICATION   T.L.C. (Tender, Loving Care)

↓   ↓

DIALOGUE   CONCERN

↓   ↓

ENCOUNTER   CONSIDERATION

↓   ↓

ACCEPTANCE   SERVICE

point out its history? If I let you be different, my ears may open and enable me to hear you, even if only enough to let some meanings in. I may be able to start listening to your ideas about serving, about operating on a team, even about changing my operation.

LISTENING: This is the Creative Listening that puts power into people by lending them an ear, and as we shall see, listening occupies some 45 per cent of our verbal time.

All day long we play tapes in our heads: on the highway, the bus, the office, every time we're alone we endlessly splice, mend, change, and add to that continuous stream we call consciousness. We talk to ourselves constantly, and some day we *have* to get some of that tape on the air—or burst!

Carlos Casteneda has Don Juan, the Indian shaman, tell him that we talk to ourselves in order to maintain our world with our internal talk. He seems to find it significant for listening that we have ears that go a bit unusued:

> Whenever we finish talking to ourselves the world is always as it should be. We renew it, we kindle it with life, we uphold it with our internal talk. Not only that, but we also choose our paths as we talk to ourselves. Thus we repeat the same choices over and over until the day we die, because we keep on repeating the same internal talk until the day we die . . . a warrior is aware of this and tries to stop his talking . . . by using your ears to take some of the burden from your eyes ("A Separate Reality . . . Conversations with Don Juan").

The economy of Christian love asks us to *listen* to each other —"As I have loved you," is the way Jesus put it—for He listened, and listens us now into love. Watch out for this listening, though. It's dangerous. We, as listeners, may actually *hear* the other, and be challenged to change: our ideas, feelings, values. For, as we listen, power grows in the speaker and the listener. The Spirit within each of us stirs in loving recognition, sending and receiving meaning.

Again, though, let's listen to the music (nonverbal communication) as well as the words of a fellow member. Note the body-style, pain in the eyes, change of color—tiny signals of where my friend is. So when you answer, answer the music first; don't snatch at the words. Watch, rather, what the tone of voice, the face, the eyebrows are saying.

How hard sometimes not to let our own eyes and tone wound those we serve, even as we try to read their feelings. Only letting the Spirit within us take over the responding can keep us kind—and yet honest. And finally the Spirit permits the heart of the other to respond where the pain is: the deepest need beyond the superficial need we sometimes try to assist.

AWARENESS: This creative, power-putting-listening leads to awareness: the other becomes established in me as a person. We neither psychoanalyze nor probe, but let the other feel what s/he feels. We proceed gradually on the High Road to a deeper grasp of how the other thinks and feels. Indispensable for development of powers of influence and for the coordination of a team; team cohesion will not happen without the honest manifestation of feeling, and the circle can facilitate it.

UNDERSTANDING: When we understand, we stand under —and look up. Up, with respect. The other is a unique expression of God's creative love. Sometimes a bit *too* unique for us, though! Yet someone with a mission, even the incredible mission of telling us something about ourselves. She may have for us a piece of good news. Listening for her/his meaning leads to the communication of meaning, the goal of our working on team: to communicate the good news of God's love.

COMMUNICATION: Communication happens when I know what you mean and you know what I mean, not just what I say. When you don't know what I mean, ask, but with the right accent on the right words, of course. Your friend will be reading your nonverbal (music) more than your words. So ask for meaning gently, humbly, remembering the See-Level ticking off your difference that can help you misunderstand the message. Be willing to risk the encounter for the joy of meanings meeting. Try using "Restatement" (below) and "Perception-Check" as well.

DIALOGUE: Once we get meanings flowing, dialogue begins: a flow and response of meanings, a nutritious activity—we feed each other, with meaning. We're giving, too, acceptance and trust, the two pillars of communion, supporting the bridge of interpersonal relationships. Yet all the dialogue in the world will never replace the world's most potent language: our actions.

ENCOUNTER: If you've built a wall between people brick by brick, you'll have to knock it down the same way, but encounter will be the reward of that patient process. By encounter I mean that two human persons get a glimpse of the mystery of the other—but just a glimpse, for the heart of that mystery is the Spirit's preserve; we can never get there. That vital differentness, that private mystery of personality makes both of us able to have something to contribute to the total mystery of the team's being and working together. We're not loving others "for God," but finding God in the very encounter of hearts sharing God.

ACCEPTANCE: And so—back to Acceptance! But after the Love Road traversed, we're miles ahead of the "letting-the-other-breathe" in the same room with us. This time we're in the stands rooting for the other—even for their difference, their uniqueness, that otherness that teaches us who we are. But the patience, the courage, the prayer needed for that road? Right! The *means* lie ready at hand—

LOVE MEANS: How to get from Acceptance to Acceptance, a suggested trip:

First of all, we'll have to *respect* the other person as that most valuable of all creatures: a human being, a child of God, no matter how heavy the disguise. That includes the right to privacy, to be different, and to disagree with us. Respect projected through our verbal and nonverbal words and music builds people and grows gifts.

Praise too, is so important. It may be the most expensive item in love's cupboard, for we hoard it so much. No doubt because the other fella' will get proud! Maybe our See-Level could yield up the deep roots of that heresy. In a world grown cold and loveless, pride is hardly a danger when depression seems to be a bit more acute than megalomania.

The disease of this our century is rather a lack of love. So praise administered artistically (the butter-knife, not the trowel) and truthfully will make us grow in observation of things to praise. And grow in love and appreciation for those we nurture.

Encouragement will help show our concern and consideration when we read the sad face, the weary walk, the tired eyes. TLC is more potent than LSD or any other picker-upper: the Tender-Loving-Care we need. Different doses for different folks supplies the acceptance and love the other needs to keep operating well.

Then comes the cut-to-the-bone: love is not love if it doesn't serve, if it can't sacrifice some time and energy for those we say we love. And some days service can be even just a smile. Otherwise, our team-dialogue might just be a lot of hot air—and not the breath of the Spirit. This serving is not slavery; it's done out of love, and its message speeds straight to the heart of the other.

When Paul describes love (*agape*: 1 Cor. 13) he puts our "Love Means" in other words. And when loving like this calls for sacrifice, brings discouragement, and sometimes little response, only that love of the Spirit's own Self in our hearts can lift us up and love *for* us just as She does the praying when we know not how to pray as we ought (Rom. 8:26).

The belief that we, too, are loved this way by the Spirit empowers us to love with that same love, and the Virtuous Circle begins. We are promised and constantly assured that God loves us. Our experience is proof of it. Christ's death confirms the fact: love to death on a cross. Loved, too, by our fellows beyond our desserts, and so, again, empowered.

The minute we know we're loved, we're first amazed, then begin to feel a marvelous unaccustomed security, and begin to relax. From what? The Rat Race—the mad rush to acquire the needed stroking to keep us ticking—praise, encouragement, respect, TLC, etc. You recognize the Love Means. Just ask yourself if you believe you need to be loved. You do? I do, too; so hang on to that for a minute.

Let's look back at that definition of the Rat Race: not your daily schedule or the freeway, but the race to get the strokes you need along with every other member on the team. Abraham Maslow insists that love deficiency is as bad for us as salt deficiency.

We all just agreed that we need to be loved, and Paul says, "Love is tender, is kind, envieth not." The Love Means says, Love is respect, encouragement, TLC. So, if we don't get that stuff, we have to play games to get it—and most dangerously: very often we do it *unconsciously*.

VIRTUOUS   CIRCLE

Loved   *Loving*

Secure   *Radiate*

Relaxed

Rat Race

Circle #3

Have you ever lived with anybody who was playing games to get praise, encouragement, acknowledgment? If you have, you know how widespread this particular Rat Race could be.

But if we're getting those things, we don't have to play games. Just think of the time and energy saved—to serve others. To love and serve and so—to be happy—a result never achieved through direct intention, but as a delightful bouquet of "other-centered" action. And so WE radiate. What? What we're getting: respect, praise, encouragement, etc. In a Virtuous Circle, a divine economy, taught us by the Master-Servant, Jesus: "as I have loved you."

I suppose what really happens is that we become lovers. We *give* to others Paul's list—respect, encouragement, acceptance—because in the circle of the team, we're getting them. When we become people-feeders like this, giving love and acceptance received from the Spirit for giving, we become sharers, lovers. A "loving person" might be the basic definition of an apostle: radiating, shining out the Spirit's light and love—*agape*.

To love someone is to bid him to live, invite him to grow. Since people don't have the courage to mature unless someone has faith in them, *they stopped developing*—they have to be loved very deeply and very boldly before they dare appear humble and kind, affectionate, sincere and vulnerable.[29]

The Virtuous Circle above (p. 65) tried to describe that process of enabling in psychological language. We'll see its theological implications below in the Gifted-Circle (p. 67).

Thus, love is the deepest form of motivation for change of heart. It is healing in itself and can create team. As team members we're striving for Paul's "hold fast to the truth and grow up completely *through love* to Him who is the head, Christ. Through Him the whole body, solidly joined together by every supporting ligament, grows with *the proper functioning of each single member* and so builds itself up by *love*" (Eph. 4:15-16).

I feel that this Come-Full-Circle in love is analogously a picture of the Spirit's manifesting power and love in our lives through the gifts. Not in a natural-supernatural dichotomy, but radiating in and through the tissue of our daily feelings, thoughts, acts, desires, and loves, so that the human person is the dynamic agent of the Spirit's action in the world, continuing the serving of Jesus who promised to send us his Spirit.

The Deepest Foundation of Team and Personal Motivation: LOVED AND EMPOWERED BY THE SPIRIT

The psychological process (of being loved into loving) let us radiate what we had received: respect, praise, encouragement, etc., and the theological dimensions of that same process (the Gifted Circle) delineates the dynamic of the Spirit's empowering us for sharing.

In it we try to draw together some strands of the "who" and the "what" of Team-Service. We see ourselves as chipped-edge sharers, incredibly loved into power through *agape,* the Spirit's highest Gift, which is Herself: "God hath first loved us."

This gift of love, this gift of being loved, allows us to relax from the need to be God. We can proceed to the integration of per-

Gifted Circle

sonality, to wholeness, because God's role in our lives is clear. Other women, other men don't threaten us, nor will we be jealous of their talents, for their talents belong to all of us. Their gifts are for the community, so when I say "Yes" to their tested gifts, I say "Yes" to God.

Leaning back in the arms of the Spirit, we experience the transforming of our life-energies under the motivation of the goal: to respond with love to Love. This experience and continuing process of conversion proceeds intellectually, emotionally, religiously, and in our moral life as well. So it leads to *Self-Integration*, because it:

(1) straightens out my Goals and, so, my Roles;
(2) affirms who I am—my identity—a loved person;
(3) gives me peace and serenity: see Gifted Circle;
(4) increases my faith;
(5) leads to deeper acceptance of myself and others as gifts for the team which permits serving together;
(6) puts me on the road to saying "we"—the goal of Christian Community.

Practical Consequences for Team Serving

Serving viewed in this light leaps into sharper focus as *sharing*: receiving and giving of the Spirit through presence and serving. On the team we function equally well whether *receiving* or *fostering* the gifts of others or polishing our own. In serving we're involved in transforming life-energy under the motivating love of the Spirit, pursuing the goal of the People of God: *the transformation of the world in Christ through the Spirit in justice, peace, and love.*

The most fantastic joy of our lives can become experiencing ourselves as a *means* for that goal through the mutual discerning and growing of others' and our *gifts* for the community, each one relaxing into the security of knowing that the greatest of gifts is *love*, which is ours, all of us, no matter what our particular gifts.

What will motivate us, then, at the deepest of all levels for team serving? Our adherence to that goal and that task. With that vision, our personal goals can sometimes die in the fire of the Paschal Mystery because we know they will be transformed in that dying into rising in the *Team-Sum* of gifts used for serving need.

In the hands of the Spirit, team members need not fear for their gifts. They will find development and fruition in the Spirit's "real" time.

THE ORDER OF EMPOWERING (BELOVED-ING):
Motivation

1. I accept myself as Loved: I am loved, so, I AM.
2. I accept myself as I am: chipped and loved and reconciled.
3. I accept others as they are: chipped and loved and reconciled.
4. I accept LOVE Herself. I can now give God God, so:
5. I can now LOVE in turn, and in re-turn: I can *give* God to you.

To serve on a team will mean asking for, growing in, practicing *love* for one another, especially through respecting, accepting, and obeying the Spirit's *bestowal* of abilities, opposing the culture's negative view of our humanity. Practically speaking, we are back to the key concept of *communication* by which we express, articulate, and listen to those gifts in ourselves and others. Communication is the life-blood of the team, so let's see how it relates to our concept of what team means.

COMMUNICATION: Life-Blood of the Team

"But nobody told me!" "When did we decide about that?" Sure-fire signals that it's not working: our communications system! Goals will be better realized if we all know about them. That means that our team decides and implements a *method* of letting the team know where we are, what we're doing, and what we mean by what we say and do. So, some training in communication is a "must."

Here's where our goal-setting, deciding, and buying what the team is really about comes into play. If we are not a corporation, but rather a "community-of-faith serving" then we are witnesses, models of what we are about: we define what it is to "Imitate God" by how we act. We'll need to share our faith with one another, facilitated by a moderator, perhaps, in a live-in weekend or like time together.

For this reason, some beginning teams use a tentative "Lab-

Period" for working together to try out the *shared* dimensions of team we looked at above. Within six months to a year, they get a good idea of who has what it takes to be a part of a "collegial" community:

(1) openness;
(2) listening-power;
(3) dedication to the common goal;
(4) competence to serve;
(5) awareness of feelings in self and others;
(6) flexibility to work and (possibly) live with others;
(7) eagerness to grow through interaction;
(8) willingness to receive gifts from others;
(9) willingness to combine individual and group goals if sacrifice is needed;
(10) a *big fat sense of humor*! (Why take life so seriously? We'll never get out of it alive!)

The orientation weekend that precedes this lab-period (if the team so chooses) could feature two or three sessions on communications-skills as lubrication for team-machine. What could follow is vital: a commitment to growing awareness of the *need* to communicate. Which means I honestly try to understand what you mean and you try to do the same for me. If our meanings get across, we've communicated. "Oh, I know what you mean!" = the sweetest words you'll hear on the team.

When we start out cold (all of us new to one another) or semi-cold (some of us know one another), let's fight assumptions. Admit that we actually need to know much more about us. *The Johari Window*[30] is a good prop or X-ray of how much we're aware of at the start of being team. And how we *want* to look in awareness of each other at the finish (three years from now when we're rolling?).

Our *goal* becomes enlarging Box I, what we all know, and decreasing Boxes II and III, hidden areas. Box IV will always be an area of consideration, but it, too, can be reduced through the illuminator-lubricator called:

THE JOHARI WINDOW: AN X-RAY FOR *AWARENESS:*
How much do we know?

Box I: Information known to all of us (public self; free activity)
Box II: Blind to you; known by others (blind spot of yours)
Box III: Blind to others; known by you (private self; hidden area)
Box IV: Blind to all of us (unknown activity area: future of "us"?)

WHEN OUR TEAM *BEGINS*,
WE LOOK SOMETHING LIKE THIS:

I	II
III	IV

THREE YEARS FROM NOW,
WE HOPE WE'LL LOOK LIKE THIS:

I (increase)	II
III (decrease)	IV

COMMUNICATIONS-MINDEDNESS: We "think about"
and *know how to* receive and send meaning

If we want to enlarge the boundaries of our shared knowledge, let's go to work on *communication*, then, as *prime requisite* for team serving.

First, of course, we'll always examine our assumptions—at the weekly staff meeting, weekends, prayer sessions, etc. Let's *each* take responsibility for getting information, data, feelings, announcements around the group to *each* member.

We can use:

(1) *Person:* visit one another at work, pray with, eat with, fun with each other.

(2) *Paper:* notes, bulletins (vital), written and printed announcements, letters, copies of everything for everybody—don't ASSUME!

(3) *Phone:* very effective when well used (ask a campaign manager)—for esprit de corps, quick announcements of changes in plans, schedule, assignment, in order to avoid:

THE OBSTACLES TO COMMUNICATION:
Those Human Basics Again

(1) *Privacy of Experience.* You cannot HAVE another member's experience, or she, yours. Your "events" are incommunicable because uniquely your own. When we try to share them, we only play a part of the tape in our heads. Remember the other fellow doesn't have the rest of that tape to make sense out of what you say—to YOU! The reason, of course, is:

(2) *Difference: the SEE-LEVEL.* Sometimes when we think we're having a personality problem in trying to communicate, just let's take our foot off the other's See-Level. We're probably standing on somebody's culture, educational background, wounded experience, environmental bump, or disappointed expectations—and it's tweaking! Gives us perspective to step back in head and heart and question our approach. Cooler than counting ten!

(3) *Behavioral Feedback.* We need one another to KNOW how we affect the work, people, the team: rear and side-view mirrors to get our serving on the road. To operate in a human way, we

need others to give us that picture of HOW we come on. If the team is not committed to and able to express feelings, no feedback. So no correction of our cybernetic system, no trust or risk—and eventually, no growth. Team goes down drain.

Expressing disagreement is a form of communication. It may well mean members' being honest enough to say what they really feel or think. Instead of being afraid of disagreement, the team will welcome it and use it constructively: to build feeling-expression, more trust, and more risk-taking IN the team meeting and not after. When a team begins to have its REAL meeting out in the hall after the meeting, it's time to take the temperature and awaken some awareness of where to iron out the kinks in communicating honest difference, because our culture often fights expressing disagreement.

If the trust level is low, if people begin to feel queasy about sharing the dimensions above, somebody has to break the ice and prayerfully and carefully bring the situation to team's attention. They know it anyhow. But the ice-breaker must get it out on the table. Then honesty, information, prayer can all air the problem. If not, dig into the following for a possible cause of non-sharing IN the meeting: *HILDDA* is its name:

(1) HIDDEN AGENDAS:[31] the secret purposes of each person in the room can hinder communication. My individual goals may be fighting the team agenda. Fear and intolerance rear ugly heads.

(2) IMAGES: "I can't hear what you're saying because of what I expect you to say." Try to filter out the prejudices and distorted set pictures (stereotypes) you might have built up of another member. Get your feelings out about it, and the image may go "Pop!"

(3) LANGUAGE: Our words don't mean. *We* mean the words, but the listeners have a different See-Level and translate words through their unique filter. So checking through *restatement* and *perception check* might be needed. Don't ever be afraid to simply ask: "What did you mean by _____?" It's a compliment; it means you really want to know what they think. More, you *believe* they think! Just be careful in a tight spot where you put the *accent* on those words!

After all, in verbal communication, we are exchanging a

shared system of symbols. Most often, few of us has ever had formal training in listening; yet communication involves sending and receiving *meaning*, with "Listening" accounting for the major part of that "Receiving."

Next time you're in a one-to-one conversation, can you catch yourself waiting for the other to finish so that you can begin speaking? This is called "listening" by most of us! Whereas the "Creative Listening" we need on the team makes our hungry ego *fast* while we make ourselves *present* to the other's ideas and feelings. To listen deeply and patiently gradually trains out of us the need to interrupt because we're not really listening but only rebutting, reacting, and so failing to receive meaning.

Studies have shown that we spend seven out of every ten waking minutes of our lives in some kind of verbal communication, and in these proportions:

WORDS	= SPEAKING	= 30%	of those 7 minutes
"	= WRITING	= 9%	" "
"	= READING	= 16%	" "
"	= LISTENING	= 45%	" "

No wonder communication (sending and receiving meaning, with listening the major factor) is the number-one-problem both on the team and in married life as well. The life of the team or the family is based on a system of sending and receiving meaning. Verbal communication is a great part of that pattern. It's the *words*.

Of course, nonverbal communication is sometimes even more important: the expression, tone of voice, body-style, eyebrows! Where we sit, how we stand, our walk—all these things radiate meaning. Think how effective and meaningful an embrace can be —or a kiss! Judas thought so, too. Remember, it's the *music*.

(4) DEFENSIVENESS: If I hear you, I may have to change . . . that is, if I listen! We can only accept change if we see it as an enhancement of ourselves in some way. Our need for affirmation is always ticking—our concern for our own being—and if someone is standing on our See-Level, our ears just fold. We can't hear a thing they say. We have to accept and respect this deep-seated need in ourselves and others and deal with it. Awareness plus

prayer to the Spirit and kindly openness can help surface the threat caused by the challenge to change—if we're listening.

So defensiveness can lead to another "D": *denial.* "There's no problem!" "What do you MEAN? *I'm* not threatened!" Denial is Defense, of course, against the threat of having to change, that built-in risk of communicating.

Defense number two many of us use to fend off the risk of change: *projection.* "*He* really has problems!" "Who does *she* think she is?" "I wonder when she had her last check-up?" The problem can't be with *us* (because we can't cope with the need to change right now) so we project the issue onto somebody else— usually the person who might have roused the fearsome need to change.

(5) ANXIETY compounded of personal worries, fears about the agenda, about some relationship in the group, about our individual roles. They all cause us to lose the quiet attentiveness that can make the team meeting move and communication happen. If we keep our hearts turned to the wisdom and insight of the Spirit moving about our group, anxieties have a way of subsiding as we get a chance to marvel at the power and light exuded—especially if we turn down the smoke and heat of worry and fear.

HELPFUL HINTS: Communication as Art Form

When meaning comes to us, an *event* takes place inside us. We've been looking at the problems caused when we try to get that unique event (filtered through *our* unique See-Level) OUT to somebody else. They will certainly filter our story through *their* See-Level—another translation of our translation! Hopeless?

No, thank God for the miracle that we can communicate at all! Imagine, we *can* share with someone else a purely personal unique event uniquely and privately experienced by us. We just go ahead and create another event to share with our team member. Remember, it's NOT what we've experienced—and it's NOT what happened inside *us*. This is a *new thing* entirely. That's what we do when we send or receive meaning. Then we wonder why misunderstanding is par for the course! Why not wonder that we *can* communicate—and find it our greatest human joy?

Usually we use three ways to communicate with another person:

1 Touch :

(1) We actually *touch* the other in some way:

handshake
pat
slap—blow
embrace

2 Move :

(2) We *move* some part of us, for instance:

nod our heads
smile
cry—frown—scowl
raise an arm
wave a hand
point a finger
widen or wink our eyes

³Symbol :

(3) We use *symbols* (happenings) taking the place of what we experienced within:

sounds: we impinge upon the auditory power of the other

we strike the ear—like

"Hello-o-o!!"

sight: we create changes or pictures or patterns *in* something so that they become a happening for the neighbor—like a **word**

An educated adult uses about two thousand words per day. Of these, the five hundred most frequently used have fourteen thousand dictionary definitions. Imagine how little equipment this is to translate the flood of experience pouring over us every minute! Each poor word has to be stretched—and then stretched—to cover an enormous range of meanings. So people have to mean and twist the words available for their meaning-conveying to others. It becomes silly, then, to ask: what does this word mean?

In all our communication, the question is: "What do *you* mean?" Too often we ask life what *it* means: "What is the meaning of life?" And all the time life is asking us what *we* mean, we who are doing the living.

That leads us to the painful but very interesting discovery (if we really begin to listen to ourselves speaking) that *we* are making major assumptions in our sending and receiving messages, like:

(1) assuming that everybody knows what *we're* talking about (they don't; they are translating through See-Levels);

(2) assuming that we know what *others* are saying without checking (Restatement and Perception Check, below p. 78);

(3) assuming that *we* know what *we're* talking about (Using the checklist below can give us the fascinating experience, if we listen closely next time we talk, of realizing that we actually don't—not always!)

Those three assumptions corrected, we're free to pay attention, to listen hard enough, and to keep some things in mind like:

(1) All our receiving and sending meaning is limited and fragmentary and a *translation*.

(2) Every time we speak or write we're translating our own experience.

(3) Words don't mean, people mean words.

(4) The same word can have opposite meanings to different people.

(5) Always ask for meanings if you don't understand.

(6) When we hear "They" said it, always ask "who?"

(7) Always check *what* was said at firsthand. Forget it, if it's what somebody *thinks* somebody else said.

(8) Remember that when we speak we only play out loud a tiny piece of our tape. We don't assume everybody else knows the whole thing.

(9) Ask the Spirit to speak in our words and translate for us the words of others; the Spirit knows what we *and* they mean!

(10) Thinking and praying are forms of communication, too: with our *Self* and the *Spirit*.

(11) Let people say whatever they want to say. If it hurts our See-Level, check why. It's a chance to grow.

(12) When threatened, let's relax, seek for truth, ask for more facts, examples, in an open, inquiring way rather than thundering, "NO!" and beginning our rebuttal.

(13) We all hate negative feedback about ourselves, but still welcome it as a compliment. It means somebody thinks we are open enough to hear it; few of us get the chance.

Or, be a bit more practical, and try out the scheme below in your teamwork to find out if you've "heard" correctly. Then practice often:

TO HELP *YOU* UNDERSTAND *THEM:* LEARN TO *LISTEN*—USE:

	I (when they have finished speaking)
	RESTATEMENT of what s(he) *said*
IDEAS (What they *said*)	(A) Use only your own words; don't just repeat theirs: Words don't mean, people mean words.
	(B) Be more specific; translate their general statement through an example: don't settle for what you don't understand.
	II and:
	PERCEPTION CHECK (of feelings you observed)
FEELINGS (How they seemed to you to *feel*)	(A) Just label the feeling: "you seemed hurt, happy, bored, etc."
	(B) Express neither approval nor disapproval in your voice, eyes, words; watch your *nonverbal music*!

When it all gets too much, just mumble to yourself: "I know you believe you understand what you think I said, but I am not sure you realize that what you heard is not what I meant."

SUMMARY

People who wish to serve together may want to do that serving on a team. To do so, we have seen that they will need a SHARED UNDERSTANDING (meaning) of Serving through:

Their common "Why": (Goal, Purpose: Section I)

Their common "Who": (Servants with Gifts and Limitations: Section II)

Their common "What": (Sharing of Abilities: Receiving and Giving of Gifts: Section IV)

When they begin to implement that common understanding on a team, the "what" of Team Serving (two or three gathered together in His name) calls for communication, the receiving and sending of *meaning* as tool for the receiving and sending of abilities, talents, and energies, called *sharing*.

Communication cannot happen at the deepest levels unless the team members agree upon a common *theory* of why they do what they do and a *common theology* (God is Chair-Person of the team so we obey God's decisions about who exercises which gifts). Then that common viewpoint and attitude is lived out in practice through:

A Shared Process (experiencing the movement from acknowledging their own limitations to helping others)

A Shared Sociology (learning the dynamics of the "groupness" of being a team)

A Shared Situation (becoming aware that this moment in history calls for healing and reconciliation of our alienation in sex, race, creed, etc.)

A Shared Motivation (loved into power, love, and enthusiasm by the empowering love of God)

This common *experience* of process, groupness, situation, motivation, and shared understanding is based upon our common theology, tested daily in the field of actual sharing of abilities in any set of relationships: society, business, government, education, industry, or church. But without the practice of the art of communication, the team still may fail to develop its rich potential.

Communication, then, is the constant concern of the team.

For this reason, I've mentioned it in various ways and in various places in this text. Though the communication I envisaged for the team is helped, indeed, by good techniques (as we shall see in the section following), its most potent practice stems from the team's listening to the Spirit in their own hearts and in the lives of others.

This kind of listening-deeply implies listening breathlessly—holding back our ego-hungry selves in daily practice of a period of serenity and perspective in which we shut off the Niagara Falls constantly pouring over our consciousness. We still the "drunken monkey" chattering and banging against the walls of our skull-cage. In a word, we take time to listen to the Spirit in our own hearts.

Members of the team, experiencing their own need-of-help daily in trying to serve others, may gradually be drawn to set aside each day a time to be alone with self and God. This would mean: (1) *deciding* to take such time (seeing this time as a value-priority); (2) *taking time* to be alone, letting the Spirit in on our channels. tuning out the picture, and the static, and resting in God; (3) *shutting up* and letting God speak to us, and gradually, responding to God in intimate conversation.

The practice of this type of communication with God ensures that our *social* receiving and sending of meaning with others will be gradually touched with serenity and vision too. Slowly, by always turning to God to *hear* inspirations, insights, nudges, we learn to relax into His plan, buy His method, radiate His viewpoint, and love with His love. Then when the team comes *together* to listen to God together (liturgy, worship, community) they bring their individual word, message, insight from the Spirit to share for the total growth of the team.

> *The world is the person unknown to me whom I allow to minister to me. It is the cup of cold water not only given but received in Jesus' name (Karl Olsson in* Faith/at/Work*).*

VI. "FIELDS-WHITE": THE WHERE OF TEAM

When anyone is joined to Christ s(he) is a new being; the old is gone, the new has come. All this is done by God who through Christ changed us from enemies into his friends, and gave us the task of making others his friends also. Our message is that God was making friends of all through Christ. God did not keep an account of their sins against them, and he has given us the message of how he makes them his friends (2 Corinthians 5).

In Chapter VII, The HOW of Team (Enabling Change), we will start with insistence on good technology and finally roll into the Virtuous and Gifted Circles to the chief "how," the highest art of team: loving obedience to the Spirit's call and gifts empowering us joyfully into service, no matter what our life-role or style.

This common viewpoint of service has heavy implications for the "where" of team today. Where will we use such a theology and circular-method in serving together in the real world of burning human need? I believe the answers imply a circular-model of "church" (and of most of society's future structures) striving to balance institutional and individual gifts.

Some Operating Factors

But how can teams of nonexperts hope to effect change, when changing social structures is a painfully long, slow, frustrating process? Where can they find a spot to use their gifts? The early Christians, confronting with their way-to-live the structure of the Roman Empire, may have felt the same way. However, the following factors are usually involved:

1. Real human need will call for response.

2. Gifts discovered in serving dictate field of action.
3. Use (1) and (2) above in *prayerful* searching with the Spirit to make our *decision* about the *where*.
4. Relax, after choice, since we're not God, and can call upon resources outside our group.

Once this is decided, we'll have to take into account elementary principles of operation like: C^2OR^2P—to give it *body*:

1. CONSULTATION:	Ask for advice, help, opinions, within and outside our team: civic, professional, private.
2. COALITION:	Ally ourselves with like-goaled groups, avoid duplication, gladly abolishing ourselves and joining another team if that's what the situation and the Spirit call for.
3. ORGANIZATION:	Treated fully above: knowledge of and responsible use of structure.
4. REFERRAL:	Limit our scope according to our resources, gifts, and goals, handing over to others parts we can't handle.
5. REPRESENTATION:	Of the team, by the team, for the team *and* of all those they serve on all boards, decision-making committees, etc.
6. PARTICIPATION:	SHARING IN a) responsibility for roles and resources; b) decision-making on proper levels; c) rewards and sufferings (necessary outcome of shared serving and risk-taking).

Shape and Constituency of "Where" (TEAM—NOT A "FAMILY")

No matter which area of human need we choose to address, note that the SHAPE of service remains the same: *circularity* is the model at this historical moment. And why? Simply because we need structures today that *disperse power* and concentrate on *human development.* We've mentioned reasons for this in "why" above, but in choosing areas of service, we need to emphasize it again. Pyramid is past. Circle is in.

The fact leads us to discuss what may have been an assumption for us right along: the actual make-up and constitution of a serving team. A structure that shares power and grows people is not the traditional "family" model. In fact, the ideal of "family" is a booby-trap for teamwork. The family model implies a Big Daddy or Mommy, and, of course, a bunch of kids. This model has not particularly strengthened the collegial structure of religious orders, but adoption of a real team model may help renew them. I believe this to be true because the principles above:

$$C^2OR^2P = \begin{cases} \text{CONSULTATION} \\ \text{COALITION} \\ \text{ORGANIZATION} \\ \text{REFERRAL and REPRESENTATION} \\ \text{PARTICIPATION} \end{cases}$$

do not fit the traditional family model. The team is not parent-oriented, but deals in horizontal relationships facilitated by the circular model based on the Spirit's power given for the community and team: *koinonia* (fellowship). This implies *people* striving for maturity, wholeness, responsibility, and fulfillment of life-vocations through service and sharing: a healthy psychological model as well. "People" means married men and women, single men and women, teen-agers, ordained and not ordained. Sex and age are not important criteria; a call and gifts for service are.

The circular model also helps do away with the *emotional expectations* laid on a group if they are expected to relate to one another as family. They are not a family, and the sooner they settle that, the better and the faster they can get to work taking their own responsibility, sharing talents, energy, love and affection, but not under the compulsion that each is expected to relate intimately with everybody. Friendship is the goal, but there is no necessity for familial intimacy. It may or may not occur depending upon the Spirit's ordering of events.

Team members are co-servers whose goal is friendship, for

friendship is, we earnestly hope, the aim of the team. We are trying to develop the relationship of one person to another under the
guidance of the Spirit which can make us one. Finally, we hope,
there will be neither male nor female, slave nor free, but all will be
one in Christ (Gal. 3:28).

> Friendship
> is an exchange of love,
> the complete
>   personal
>   involvement
> of two people
> who are so free
> in their self-possession
> that they can
> emote adequately
> the appropriate
>   adult
>   responses.
> Only a person
> who is integrated enough
> to be comfortable
> in solitude
> and to live productively
> without a friend
> has the vitality
> really to love warmly
>   and
>   humanly
> in friendship.
>
> To love another
> in friendship
> is to give
> of oneself,
> the best one has,
> in such a way that
> freedom

is not lost
nor personal integrity
violated.
To love and respect
a friend
means to care so much about him
that one
could do nothing
really to hurt him
or oneself (Louis Evely).

Role-Oriented through Collegial Gifts

Still, members do have different Roles in the on-going work of the team and its corporate life. These Functional Roles are usually grouped under the headings of:

1. *Group Task Roles:* concerning the job the team is undertaking. It helps the team-effort to achieve its goals, although each member may enact more than one or a range of them in different sessions or given situations:

(a) *Initiator-contributor*—suggests or proposes to group new ideas or a changed way of regarding the problem. May be solution or way of handling trouble, or new way of organizing group for task ahead.

(b) *Information seeker*—asks for clarification of suggestions, for authoritative information and facts pertinent to the problem discussed.

(c) *Opinion seeker*—asks not so much for facts but for clarification of values pertinent to what group is trying to do, or values involved in suggestions given.

(d) *Information giver*—offers facts which are "authoritative" or relates own experience.

(e) *Opinion giver*—states own belief in regard to a suggestion made: wants to push what should become the group's view of pertinent values, not just facts or information.

(f) *Elaborator*—spells out examples of suggestions given, or tries to deduce how it would work.

(g) *Coordinator*—shows relationships among various ideas

and suggestions; tries to pull ideas together.

(h) *Orienter*—defines the position of group with respect to its goal by summarizing, or raises questions about group-direction.

2. *Group Building and Maintenance Roles:* to get the group to function *as group*, designed to change/maintain the team's way of working, providing cohesion as a team:

(a) *Encourager*—praises, agrees with, accepts contributions of others; warmth in attitude toward members; pushes for solidarity of group.

(b) *Harmonizer*—mediates differences between other members, relieves tension in conflicts through jesting.

(c) *Compromiser*—operates within a conflict in which his/her idea is involved; may yield, admit error, or may come half-way to move along with the group.

(d) *Standard setter*—expresses standards for group to try to achieve in its functioning.

(e) *Gate-keeper*—expediter, attempts to keep communication channels open by encouraging others: "We haven't heard from Tim yet."

(f) *Group-observer*—keeps records of aspects of group process and feeds data with proposed interpretations into group's evaluation of its own procedures.

(g) *Follower*—goes along with the movement of the group.

3. *Individual Roles:* attempts by members of group to satisfy individual needs irrelevant to the group task and *perhaps* negatively oriented to group-building:

(a) *Aggressor*—may express disapproval of others, acts, feelings, or show envy toward others by trying to take credit for ideas, etc.

(b) *Blocker*—tends to be stubbornly resistant, opposing without much reason.

(c) *Recognition-seeker*—works to call attention to self, boasting, acting in unusual ways, struggling to be out of an "inferior" position in discussion, etc.

(d) *Self-confessor*—uses the chance for an audience which the group provides to express "feeling," "insight," "ideology" about self (usually to get sympathy).

(e) *Playboy/girl*—makes display of lack of involvement in group: cynicism, horse-play.
(f) *Dominator*—tries to assert authority or superiority in manipulating group or members of group: through flattery, superior status, giving directions, interrupting, etc.
(g) *Help-seeker*—tries for sympathy (response from group) through expressing insecurity, personal confusion, or depreciation of self beyond reason.

Individual vs. Team Roles

If we buy the circular-model, Individual Roles, negatively oriented, have to confront squarely *requirements* for maintaining the Task and the Cohesion Roles of the group. When we looked at these above we saw them from the angle of how the team would supply these needs to the team members. In the face of Individual Roles working against the group task, let's look at them now from the side of the individual team-member trying to discover if and how a "gift-become-role" relates to where the team works.

First of all, the team-need for *achievement*, so strongly pushed by our individual needs as well. Let's ask some questions to juxtapose personal-need and team-characteristic and clarify this concept. The answers help individuals decide if their gifts fit the work of the team or not. These questions also help the team discern about individual members' achievement. Sharing those answers with them and the team helps the group decide about and evaluate each one's work.

Once the three needs below: achievement, power, and affiliation are faced, acknowledged, and worked through, the question of where to serve is not such a problem. A group that keeps working through these questions is open and ready for whatever area the Spirit opens up through people, geography, and events.

Varieties of Roles, Gifts, and Need

A. You, your accustomed Role, your Gifts, and the NEED FOR ACHIEVEMENT:

Section A

_____ 1. When you start a task, do you stick with it?

_____ 2. Do you try to find out how you are doing, and do you try to get as much *feedback* as possible?

_____ 3. How do you respond to difficult, challenging situations?

_____ 4. Do you work better when there is a deadline or some other challenge involved?

_____ 5. Are you eager to accept responsibility?

_____ 6. When you are given responsibility, do you set (and meet) measurable standards of high performance?

B. You, your accustomed Role, your Gifts, and the NEED FOR POWER (to control environment, people, events, self):

Section B

_____ 1. Do you seem to enjoy a good argument?

_____ 2. Do you seek positions of authority where you can give orders, rather than take them? Do you try to take over?

_____ 3. Are status symbols especially important to you, and do you use them to gain influence over others?

_____ 4. Are you especially eager to be your own boss, even where you need assistance, or where joint effort is required?

C. You, your accustomed Role, your Gifts, and the NEED FOR AFFILIATION:

Section C

_____ 1. Do you seem to be uncomfortable when you are forced to work alone?

_____ 2. Do you interact with other members and go out of your way to make friends with new people?

_____ 3. Are you always involved in group projects, and are you sensitive to other people (especially when they are "mad" at you)?

_____ 4. Are you an apple-polisher, and do you try hard to get personally involved with your superiors?

Varieties of Teams = Varieties of NEED—Team is
Shaped by Need:

The team is not family, nor is it a commune. Nor need it be steering committee or a parish council. A serving team is what the task calls for. Human need is the criterion of the shape and kind of team and not vice versa. "Human-need-to-be-served" dictates the ethos, the life-style, the operation of the group of people who may want to serve together and pledge themselves to pursue a common goal with the prerequisites we've seen above.

The mistake would be to let a preconceived idea of the shape of team get in the way of what we want to do. This is what finally happened to some religious orders in the United States. Starting out serving the poor in the streets, some of us ended up being unavailable to anybody, let alone the poor, except at our time, in our way, at our hours, according to a life-style we learned to worship. And so we lost sight of our goals.

So, then, questions of living-in? living-out? same house? different houses? men *and* women? lay *or* religious? —Protestant? Catholic? Jewish? These are not real questions if we've bought a common theory of the gifts for serving. And if we let crying human need dictate our response and choice of vehicle. The Wheel of team may prove the swiftest mode of serving such need for many of us.

Stamp Out the "Laity!"

One last word before we plunge ahead into possible future areas of service. I mentioned above the advisability of dispensing with the term "laity" in the light of the commitment of all Christians and their call to use the Spirit's gifts for the community. A recent report from one national church affirmed that many unordained Christians feel themselves abandoned by the Church today for direction as to how their gifts relate to the "structure" called church and to society.

When selected groups were asked in a recent study, "How can the institutional church help you as lay people to live out the implications of your faith in your problems and in other areas?" the answer, in general, was that they hadn't the slightest idea how the Church related to them and to their problems. They were not avoiding the issue, but just not answering it directly. The consensus was that they felt the Church had little impact in their work/social lives—where the *problems* were: the human need, the areas of service.

The report, for "educational use only," showed Christians making no connection between their Christianity and their own vital roles as *agents of social change in the structures* in which they are immersed: business, government, university, church, etc. The result, then, on the feeling-level at least, is that "church" has become increasingly irrelevant to them, and they have no "vision" of their own vital role in effecting change in structures.

"Fields-White" = Areas of Need

Beneath this feeling of abandonment lie fear, frustration, and despair over the major issues of our time (Areas of Human Need) deeply operative in the church-member relationship.

1. *Human Rights:* dignity, liberty, decision-making, sharing, including food, clothing, and shelter for ALL humans: w&men, no matter which race.

2. *Peace* (and peace-education): including the task of outlawing WAR as a solution to human-differences, communications, and property problems.

3. *Poverty:* including painful reevaluation of the politico-economic system geared to the advantage of white, Western people fattening on the sweat of two-thirds of the world's people who do NOT profit from their toil in an economy geared to profit, not use, to protect property, not people.

4. *Institutional Intransigence:* including the examination of assumptions about the necessity of the SHAPE of present structures: paternalism denying *responsibility* to the worker and *accountability* to the administration or executive: the pyramid. Structures are stuck.

5. *Environmental Care:* including honest acknowledgment of our rape of resources and painful reassessment of our lived-assumptions about economic and technological development: willingness to LIMIT ourselves in many

ways: life-style, "paternal role," an attitude toward
our earth as SHARED GIFT, not limitless checking-
account.

Ours the Task and the Roles

"The harvest is great," said Jesus, "but the laborers are few"
(Jn. 3). Yet, in the course of history, we have seen those "few" effect change simply through the force of their powerful belief that
they could: "I can do all things in Him who strengthens me." And,
even if some Christians do feel themselves abandoned by the
"church," the Spirit has been doing some powerful speaking
through official pronouncements of the Church, *Mater et Magis-
tra, Pacem in Terris,* and *Populorum Progressio (Development of
Peoples)* to mention a few. So we really *have* the power: people
enspirited and empowered, plus the theological stance taken by
various churches to speak out for social change to address the
issues listed above (1-5): a philosophy and theology.

What is made clear by such documents and many social encyclicals that preceded them was finally loudly affirmed both by
Vatican II's implementation and the synods that followed it:
*Christians are again and again called to social responsibility and
social charity.* We ARE called to help solve these burning issues.
That response is a constitutive part of the life that tries to follow
Christ's WAY. In fact, following Christ is impossible without
some concern for the neighbor who is now our international-neigh-
bor as well in this our global village.

Face-to-face with these real issues of our time, we may grow
more aware of the fundamental vocation of every Christian to par-
ticipate in some way in social change, and also in our personal sets
of relationships that need healing, converting, reconciling.

The magnitude of the issues plus this basic need for change of
heart leads to our realizing that no mere rearrangement of the
pieces can effect the basic transformation our lives and structures
need. As team we are calling for the healing of our culture, our
economic life, our civilization, and not merely at the end of an era,
but in a time of painful transition after fifteen hundred years of
Christian history and theology from Augustine even until now.
This is a task that boggles the mind, but not if we rely on the

Spirit's faithful power and love and begin to use together the gifts we're literally loaded with: intelligence, imagination, creativity, unselfish love, and the galaxy of gifts for serving: healing, reconciling, sustaining, sharing.

Using our gifts, we who ARE the church will then cease to dichotomize ourselves as "we" and "them" laying the blame for our unrelatedness (our Christian and our everyday lives) on a hierarchical "them" called "church." The work-week is the arena of our social action. *We* run that world as breadwinners and those that serve.

We, too, as the team called the People of God, need to apply to ourselves as concerned people our principles: CCORRP above, taking the techniques and expertise of our daily work and *applying* them in an organized way to the issues in our own communities. We *are the link* of church-society, since we are church participating in the world.

For instance, the business world needs some help in taking responsibility for quality of life, for corporate social policy. Who will help if not the very people in that structure already striving to implement an ethical and religious value-system that can produce such quality? These are the business w&men who run the system and espouse a value-system that states Christ's criteria for receiving his approval: "Come, because:

I was hungry and you fed me; thirsty, you gave me drink, a stranger, you took me in; I was naked, and you clothed me; sick, and you visited me; in prison, and you came to me (Mt. 25:35).

We often fail to link work-life and value-system because of our self-concept and our attitudes, both stemming from the See-Level, of course. Often we don't know how to get work and values together, so we're timid about trying. Sometimes, then, we operate on *assumptions* like:

(1) We are not obliged to do anything about society's evil nor its values.
(2) The Christian religion doesn't call for making changes in society's values.

(3) Our See-Level (Culture, Education, Experience, Environment, and Expectations) may not teach us to value ethical-moral principles as operating principles in our work/social life (cf. "Watergate!").

(4) Our attitudes are often embedded in *habits* of not responding to our neighbor's need except perhaps in terms of giving money—or relegating the task to "George."

(5) Our faith need not be translated into our work at high levels of competence in regard to power, decision-making, and allocation of funds based on priorities geared to the responsible use of resources.

We can begin to deal with this problem of noninvolvement and withdrawal if like-minded people gather together in groups utilizing team techniques. They may gather according to their function in society or not. Soon some of them could be part of a team, according to their talents, but most importantly, they begin to serve more totally the institutions *of which they are a part.* This is their task and part of why they are there in the structure.

A team could provide them a supportive matrix for speaking out, community action, prayerful reflection, strategy, and tactics. In this team effort the so-called "laity" are the experts. This is *their* milieu of specialty. Consequently, the pyramidal model is displaced for them. Circularity spells sharing responsibility and accountability.[37]

Ordained people could very well be resource people on such teams—but they should carefully avoid directing them *alone.* Teams may start with the circular sharing model, but if old habits catch up with the professional or ordained members, they may soon begin to assume power and assert themselves. They may feel that *they* need to lead the team, not recognizing the circular operation of collegial structure, not using REFERRAL AND CONSULTATION as vital operating principles. They may even forget that they are "resource persons" for the Spirit's task.

In a transitional period like ours, these assertive practices can disrupt and limit the team, since our goal is to RECOVER the responsibility and sharing of unordained members. We cannot afford to turn off anyone's gift by assuming authority not given by the Spirit for the given situation. Dying to old ways can produce a beautiful rising for the total team as well as our own. The total activation of a community's gifts is surely a prize worth the effort.

Like-Functioned Groups May Become Team

If the people involved in institutional structures begin to group according to function or desire to serve need, they may become team in an organic process bridging the gap between society and church. This kind of team will develop if the need and the situation call for it. I see it as integral to the dissemination of values in structures needing major change in social responsibility, social policy, and use of power.

According to the Spirit's call to each person making up the team, it could well be started by a business woman/man concerned for such values. S(he) may contact outside resource people. As they search, think, plan, pray together, others will be attracted by the same Spirit who makes us one, and the concept of team is the next step—with all the homework above (Sections 3-6) to be gone through. Each team will operate according to *its* situation, need, etc. Adapt to the situation, but never skip the basics. Teams don't happen. They are earned through study, practice, and hard work.

Note that in this model of team, people are not removed from their daily fields of operation. They use resources to apply to needs they experience every day in their present roles in any structure. Their experience of need calls for the exercise of gifts that soon become roles. But without support, without a community to discern, help decide, share vision and action, few can long survive the heat of combat in a monolithic structure. How fundamental to this open approach to the Spirit's call in one's daily life is the undergirding of listening to the Spirit—especially in people and events.

Keep It Open! THE PARISH

I've purposely not yet even mentioned the parish as field of service for the team—just because I want to practice what I'm preaching and not *assume* that these teams we describe head straight for or grow out of the present parish. They may, indeed, according to our listening to human need. But, if we use gifts of imagination and creativity, we'll read the signs of the times. And the times are saying that present parishes don't seem to be meeting human needs. A parish is not necessarily the geographical locus for a sermon-factory called a church, but a theological reality created by the Spirit who alone makes us one. The ordained are in the parish for the *parishioners'* needs and service, not their own, except as part of a community.

That seems to be a fairly obvious principle, but given the nature of cultural-religious-ecclesial shock and flux, it's not obvious at all in some parishes. If certain forms of blindness to parishioners' needs continue, such parishes may well cease to exist.

I've seen parishes in which the minister/priest and his co-pastor are actually trying to do all the teaching, preaching, bookkeeping, planning, church-upkeep, worship services, and counseling. The end of that road is ulcers, resignation, or death. No person (or duo) can replace the gifts of a community. ✓

This sad picture is the reason why I don't assume that teams will address themselves primarily (if they want to deal with social evils listed above) to working in the present parish structure. Some parishes are working through how to involve Christians in using their gifts for the body of the church: the community. But they are too few. Their attempts are often sporadic and without a basis for continuity in that effort: *the power in residence: the so-called "laity."* These Christians are the true continuity locally and theologically of what it means to be church in society. So long as their gifts are not utilized for the parish and society, the Spirit is stifled. Saying "no" to their proven gifts is saying "no" to God. But if parishes shape up to *shared* responsibility and accountability, they survive.

However, if we take "parish" to mean "grouping according to shared vision of what it means to be Christian," then parishes are here to stay. Expressing that shared vision in action will call for many different gifted people to give *their* piece of good news, to give feedback to one another, to help say yes/no to one another's gifts, to listen together, to act, love, and pray together, to be Christ here and now serving His sisters and brothers.[38]

Many like-minded searchers in groups of fifty, a hundred, or more are inviting ministers/priests of either sex to share worship with them as a group. This may be the beginning of parish all over again, but not according to a geographical model. Other groups may find the geographical model most useful. Out of such growing Christian communities, teams may emerge as did once the Seven Deacons. I wish I could have sat in on THEIR meeting the first few times.

Note that we suffer from and must beware of the insidious power of the *force of habit*. Habit plus the *lack of challenge* from those who make up a structure can spell blind, unthinking confomism. In short, leading the unexamined life which is not worth living. In an age of mass communication, instant facts, TV, and world transportation, we have no right to such a life, certainly not in a time when the Gospel values of Jesus are most accessible, when the Spirit's power is unflagging. *We* are responsible for our structures.

As I see some structures working now for survival, and not their original goal, and as I see so many of us seeming closed to the cry of two-thirds of the earth's people who starve while we observe their demise on TV, I am reminded of the deafness and blindness that Jesus mentions in the Gospel.

We seem to be unable to respond with our wealth, mechanical skill, technology, communications media, organizational power to the cry of the poor. Jesus said He came that they might have the Gospel preached to them. And they asked Jesus to be cured. Do we *want* to change our own selfish structures that do not serve the poor of the world and our own country? Do we ask, too, to be cured? We may not be malicious, but we often don't know *how* to address that challenge.

Teams "Role" In

Here is where I see teams operating. Small groups of concerned people who have heard that cry can begin to reveal how they feel about what they see, hear, and smell: insensitivity to the plight of our neighbor in Africa, South America, India, etc. Even more, the poor we could see at our own door—

How? By using the talents, energies, desires to serve, of those of us who come together to share our piece of the puzzle, to come together in our spirits, first of all, finding peace, joy, and support in a team that may grow into community. Then we can come together as a mighty force to find out what God seems to be calling for through our combined powers and talents.

How can we make such change happen? That's usually thought to be the preserve of community organizers, structural analysts, economists, lawyers, politicians, etc. True, teams need all types of persons (according to their goal) to operate at these different levels, but everyone need not be a professional to be on a team. A team could comprise some professionals, of course, each following and contributing a particular skill that calls for some PARTICULAR SENSITIVITY to give us pieces of the total picture.

We know that some structures frustrated in achieving their stated goal continue to operate in the pyramidal, patriarchal fashion[39] and are closed to the cries of the needy we should be listening to. Certain classes keep RESERVED KNOWLEDGE for their own use or charge the rest of the world for its use because possibly they have neither mechanism nor imagination as to *how* to do otherwise. Further, we who are part of such structures have not been trained to question their goals or their operations.

Think about the practices of some lawyers, for example. Why must the ordinary citizen be charged and penalized, actually, because we have had a defective education? I mean that we have never been *taught* very simple basics of our legal system, now often operating contrary to citizens' best interests.

Why must the poor *pay* for the fact that the courts would grind to a shattering halt if plea-bargaining weren't used *against* them? The poor turn out to be guilty because we have not used our imagination and intelligence to question the assumptions behind an inefficient, expensive, and outdated system.

What about medicine? Should we really have to pay doctors for telling us to take a sugar pill? We're paying again for a defective *education* that failed to give us sufficient medical knowledge for normal health. Medical knowledge is NOT the sole preserve of a special class whose RESERVED KNOWLEDGE (reserved to them) strains the pocketbooks of ignorant citizens. We don't use imagination to see that each of us has gifts, only they are presently misplaced or mislaid. Along with some skills each of us could acquire enough of the basics for health without recourse to the "specialist."

If all of human knowledge belongs to ALL of us, and if knowledge is power, then we, as an exclusive-group, professional people, so-called, can not use our special learning and power to tax fellow citizens whose labor makes possible the society that nurtures our specialty.

Yet the laborer has had the sense to organize in the United States. He used the pattern: like-minded, like-functioned people unite and become power. I hope teams will operate in the same way, each following particular enspirited goals and using expertise to unite to change structures for the good of people, but that will mean:

(1) Examine the assumptions *unquestioned* in their operation.
(2) Report honestly the findings and use *all* communications media, especially TV, to disseminate them.
(3) Consult and refer for resources to address expertise to goals.
(4) Swing all of CCORRP into action:
    1. Coalition
    2. Consultation
    3. Organization
    4. Referral
    5. Representation
    6. Participation in:
        (a) decision-making power,
        (b) responsibility,
        (c) profits.

Most importantly, let's have some teams of THINKERS: philosophers, theologians, educators, poets, artists—anyone who can see clearly that the EMPEROR HAS NO CLOTHES! Think-Tanks already exist, of course, but I would ask serving teams to ensure the formation of such groups as resources to their own team or as part of it for creative alternatives and long-range planning.

Let's foster, too, the role of the PROPHET(ESS) who would say and keep saying that the EMPEROR(ESS) HAS NO CLOTHES through TV, radio, newspaper, journal, art, music, dance, as once did Aristophanes, Priscilla, Molière, Teresa, Swift, and Daniel Berrigan.

Why thinkers, prophets(esses), poets, w&men of imagination?

Because our culture has often made us captives in our own minds for the sake of law, order, and efficiency so that money might be made and property protected. Heidegger[40] felt that the way the poet responds to life is the highest measure of how we must sojourn in this world if we are to have a world and be free. For the poet comes at a sunset or a blade of grass in the spirit of "letting be" and "paying heed." S(he) summons forth out of them "what-makes-them-to-be." This gives us a world, for thus things and people can know one another and so be carried upward and together into meaning and oneness.

Jesus did this in the story-telling that we call preaching: "Consider the lilies of the field; how they grow; they labor not, neither do they spin . . ." But, note He says: *"Consider"*—think deeply in your heart with the Spirit, the Supreme Poet, who looks through us into the heart of every person and calls out: "Myself!"

So our world, with its habits and structures, goes limping on in its sad ways because WE, the habit-formers, do not "consider" in our hearts. We fail to use that *gift of imagination* or vision called faith to see beneath the corporation, government, hospital, school, or prison to the HUMAN-LIKE-ME and the DIVINE-LIKE-GOD that is the human person entrapped in the whirling of the structure-mills.

We have this gift, many of us, but it's weak, pale, under-sunned. Its throat is hoarse from long disuse. It was not for nothing that Dante called his poem THE VISION: his view of the faith-universe, and it is vision (faith-full imagination) we need to light our lamps for the doing-of-faith: to speak out against human indignity, unfreedom, and mindless conformity to a rat race of routine. The unexamined life is not only not worth living, it is also a betrayal of the faith that is in us. For it closes the blinds to the Spirit's bright vision: human persons are the supreme value; structures must "grow" them or fail to justify their existence.

Basic "WAYS TO GO" and "WHERES TO GO," in serving are "WAYS TO SEE": the vision of the meaning of human experience. Blind do-gooderism has wrought more harm than this world dreams of—especially because it was blind. So let's take very seriously a team of "Imaginers" in touch with their spirit, as resource to teams in direct service. Each group needs the other, lest the thinkers fail for lack of current data, and the do-ers operate without a vision, a first-class theory.

Theology theorizes to give us a way to think about our religious experience, to think about what's happening to our spirit. Though it reflects upon practice to discover norms, theology can still let theory substitute for reality. Both theory and practice, wedded through various kinds of teams, help keep each other honest— and functioning.

Double Vision: A Place for Teams To Operate

What if we examine the assumptions operating in some of the Operating Ends of structures today? What if we looked *beneath* the facade of STATED GOAL and demanded a finished product to prove its validity and veracity? For example, let's look at the goals of a typical prison and a typical high school. What values do they both seem to be demonstrating? Just the type of building: isolation, walls, fences, designed for efficiency, security, and surveillance.

To the extent that the message can be translated from the high school's architectural medium, the language is clear: This place VALUES regularity, order, and control over *creativity, spontaneity,* and *freedom.*[41]

Ivan Illich seemed to feel the same way, when, in totally different context, he said that the Church must affirm *play* as opposed to usefulness, *gratuity* as opposed to achievement, *spontaneity* to planning, and *messianic hope* to utopias. I mourn for the gradual death of creativity, spontaneity, and freedom in our schools, for without their vision, the nation dies, prophets speak not, no one speaks out for God, examining structural assumptions and demanding human development.

The high school may be a symbol of our failure to foster freedom and creativity. On my first trip to Vacaville Medical Prison Facility in California, I remember exclaiming how much like a high school it looked. Well it might since often there is no structure within a school for the development of creativity, spontaneity, and human development.

I mean that intelligence and imagination which characterize some of our schools are seen in their logical development in the least imaginative and most archaic structure of our society: the modern prison. Couldn't teams of informed citizens, using resource people, media, daily contacts, and influence, help our institutions develop human potential in our educational system? There is even stronger imperative for the implementation of teams in church-related groups since Christian values call for the full growth of the human personality.

Teams To Restructure Educational Systems

It seems to me that the greatest service teams might do in their local areas/parishes is to ask *what* and *how* children and young people are being taught in our schools, and why adults are not. Especially, since as Christians, our goal is to foster the growth of the gifts in one another, how can we let *human potential* be wasted? Through us the Spirit works for the transformation of the world. Ours is the task to promote it at every turn. This is our synergy, our working with God in the world. Education is the formative tool of the culture, and it *does* inculcate values whether we admit it or not.

How about enlisting the many thoughtful, concerned medical doctors, lawyers, professors, bishops, senators, executives, officials, who see this dearth of thinking power? How about asking them, through team contacts, after careful planning, to take part in ad hoc teams, in a reassessment of the TRAINING demanded for entry into their specialized field?

Then (Step Two) could educators at the various levels, e.g., first-grade experts, junior high specialists, senior high, college, and university teachers meet with the above professionals as resource persons, and together shape a graduated *mini-medical*, a *mini-legal curriculum*, etc., for elementary, for high school, for college? How about a gradually increasing (year by year) input of content and method for the knowledge of law, medicine, theology, music, a citizen would require to be free of overdependence on lawyers, courts, etc.? An "Open-Content" section of the day, each day, would also be available when young people could freely ask the questions that come alive as they grow, change, and experience fear, hate, jealousy, love, ambition, sexuality, aging, and death.

Immediately each specialty clamors for attention, for time, in an overcrowded school day. But, I would ask, "overcrowded with what?" In a nation whose size and wealth call for *international involvement and responsibility* of staggering proportions, we still must struggle to see that children learn another language. For years, proponents of a second language were told: "Let 'em learn English!" Today, a new ethnic sensibility, a new awareness of the richness of other traditions, couched in language, forces us to push for at least one more language in the child's day from the first grade on.

We sometimes refer to the Romans as the "master plumbers" of the ancient world, and see their contribution to civilization as minor compared with the riches of the Greeks and Babylonians; yet they saw to it, in their finest hour, that Roman boys learned the *koine* of the ancient world, not Latin only, but Greek. Of course, these boys were of the upper classes. They would rule the Empire.

Today we ask that *all* citizens in America be educated. Yet, all the more reason for taking into account the number of our fellow citizens whose tongue is Spanish, a realization that is all too slowly dawning on us. And what about Russian and Chinese to contact the minds and hearts, and not just the markets, of the people we need to work with for the peace of the world?

If the child's school day were filled with life-studies: how to survive in an urbanized civilization—law, medicine, theology, psychology, languages, science, math, etc.—the school would change and the child's attitude toward it. Unlike Plato, we wouldn't banish the poets from the polis, but invite them to exercise their healing arts, too, and in balanced conjunction with other modes of interpreting experience: philosophy, music, drama, and art.

A pipe-dream? Not if we honestly examine the assumptions, look at the data, and decide if the structure achieves the goal: the good of the students. I here translate that "good" as equipment to live in our society as a sufficiently educated person who can take responsibility for the community, be a real member of the same, and foster gifts therein. Again, not a dream in this our time since we, for the first time in the history of the world, possess the MEANS for disseminating information, for questioning and inculcating values, and for sharing intellectual and imaginative resources, let alone sharing the spiritual dynamism generated by this mutual sharing of one of God's greatest gifts: electronic communication, e.g., TV.

Television and Teams

Teams of men and women need to use TV time, radio time, the newspaper, and the journal (through contacts, letters, articles, scripts, trained personnel: resources of referral and consultation) to raise the level of consciousness of our need for reform in education. This could eventually spell the widening awareness of the need for a change in society and all its structures. I realize that this is a long-range approach, and I mention it first and in particular, lest it get lost in the short-range goals that push for attention from teams in pressing human-needs at this moment.

Teams working only for short-term goals will do good, but they may well slap band-aids on cancer if they do not also ally themselves, always, with groups of resource people and other organizations (coalition) mentioned above who will do their work at the proper level: theory, long-range planning, methodology, with good subsidiarity pushing work forward at *all* appropriate levels. So we would have a chance to match psychological, spiritual, and intellectual growth with the rapidity of technological and social change.

In other words, we would prepare the environment, the ecology for the growing of the gifts of all our fellow-citizens. In fact, a team could well make this its own goal of existence: to coordinate, to bring together (and to keep doing so) resource people to service, evaluate, to examine and to watch (goal-wise) our structures. Most certainly, to keep the educational system alive and growing, refusing to let it calcify from habit and false assumptions.

If *Sesame Street* could help prepare first graders *before* some children go to school, why not use TV to continue *beyond* first grade *various* types of education: law, medicine, life-problems, philosophy, theology, art, music, language at the level of the child's competence? Since children now spend hours of their growing time planted right in front of that tube, they could learn "continuously" and painlessly.

Teams could take responsibility for encouraging such programming, replacing the monopoly of another structure: *advertising*, which usurps the *use* of our vision-time, and leaves us, too often, with only our waist-lines expanded. Yet TV is the greatest teaching medium in the history of education. Why don't we question the insulting nature of its advertising and the abysmal level of content of its presentations? We hardly need the value-system perpetrated upon the public, the lowering of the level of public sensibility, refinement, and taste from the pollution-of-the-eyes many a program produces.

Strangely enough, no modern structure is so susceptible to public response and opinion as TV. Polls, questionnaires, scales, measure success by the "stretching-of-our-eyeballs" per program. Why not *use* that power to fight back and demand that we receive what we need for ourselves and our children: an intelligent, imaginative, creative, artistic use of the small screen? Otherwise, we're either getting what we want or what we deserve! A field-white for the harvest for an ecumenical, w&man team working for human values, tube-control, and high-quality education through the public medium of communication. It is both possible and practical.

Of course, such teams would consult, coordinate, organize, use coalition and contacts, and grow the gifts of others. In a huge society like ours no one is more needed than the coordinator of gifts. Teams can do this: locate, foster, bring together, encourage, and give public support to the experts who can do the designing, planning, programming, script-writing.

The secret is: we don't have to do it *ourselves*! Subsidiarity, consultation, and referral provide the resources. Ordinary competent COMMUNITY ORGANIZATION skills give the form, while the Spirit is the power and the motivation. Above all, as a team, we'll seek to discover *from* the Spirit *how* we are to proceed. We *yearn* to be *taught of God* so we *learn* to take time to become w&men of *vision*.

Finance and the Team: It Pays!

Let's look now at the money factor operative in our structures. Is it possible that the perversion of the stated goal of our legal system, "Equal Justice Under Law," stems from the over-concern of some lawyers for exorbitant fees? That the greed of some bailbondsmen and the court system at some local levels may perpetuate plea-bargaining? If other countries can do without this antiquated system, why does the United States perpetuate it? But note also the desire to change, innovate, find new models, mechanisms, and skills evident in some of our law schools.

How about the same factor operating in medical care? In hospitals, rest homes, retirement homes, wherever the system operates? Could money fed into the system by its partisans be rerouted to stress preventive medicine and incorporate the concept of total-patient-care into society and hospital services to benefit the ordinary citizen?

Could health-care institutions help to set up *education* for preventive medicine, for public-health care, through using *their* prestige on the local media? Using their powerful contacts, their wealthy resource people—pharmaceutical companies, hospital supply firms, etc. A concerted effort by nursing, medical, and health-care personnel and staff could bring to reality on commercial TV the kind of medical education all citizens need for normal healthy functioning.

We'd thereby break the monopoly of the professions on EXCLUSIVE KNOWLEDGE. And we'd help some professionals to see their specialty again as *service* to a community, not a private gold mine or game preserve.

How much mythology, superstition, and old-wives' tales could be wiped out by the clever, colorful cartoon, the graphic use of powerful media to teach anatomy, physiology, hygiene, preventive medicine and dental care! Why not this field for teams planning to USE power and finances for the GOOD of the citizen, and not only for profit? Civic teams could help organize, motivate, and activate such planning.

This is an open field for the religious orders of w&men who run many health-care facilities: to open them up to the general public's need for information, to share their staff, resources, services for such civic educational programming on TV. Most of all, to be initiators of ecumenical, man-woman teams to get a local community's structures mobilized to provide this service. Teams made up of hospital personnel could be a powerful public-relations tool reaching out with knowledge and values into the local structures, uniting business, government, church, and educational structures in pursuit of the SHARING of Reserved Knowledge with the public. They could break down antiquated structures, e.g., some hospitals as such.[42]

In this connection I would recommend that such groups (hospital or medical teams) take for study a book like Ivan Illich's *Medical Nemesis: The Expropriation of Health.* They might find it profitable to concentrate not only on his controversial analysis of our medical system, but especially on his theology of and spirituality of death and dying. These are certainly areas that require exploration on TV for all of us, given our present ignorance about them.

Most important about Illich's approach is the clear outline of the *values* from which he launches his critique of society's structures, valuable for teams doing the same whether or not they agree with his attitude. Without clear goals based on an agreed-upon value-system, the team can hardly summon the energy and enthusiasm needed to involve the public in the self-analysis needed for structural improvement.

Women and Teams

Utopian, you might say! And you're right, except for some interesting things changing in our society: the role of women, the possibility of a real value-challenge through their new power, and the possible effects, if they can listen to the Spirit as to *how* to mobilize that power into structures and operating value-systems.

When the Equal Rights Amendment passes, women will have full access to decision-making roles for the first time at executive levels, even in the federal government, let alone in the university, business, and the Church. What if women, noticing a peculiar relationship between the role of finance and some structural malaise, would decide that THEIR POWER and THEIR money will *not* perpetuate such systems?

However, equality before the law is a must before teams of women can operate, especially in the COALITIONS that will spell real structural power for value-implementation and challenging social evil, so the passage of the Equal Rights Amendment is essential.

At first, for purposes of building identity and self-concept, women will band together in totally female groups/teams: NOW, League of Women Voters, National Assembly of Women Religious, Church Women United, National Coalition of American Nuns. Gradually, however, as women move into positions of power and prestige, these groups may well swing their weight, training, and experience into ecumenical, woman-man, *inclusive* National Organization of HUMANS, Voters' League, Church People United, Leadership Conference of Religious. Better still, teams of w&men will operate within the U.S. Senate, the House of Representatives, the cabinet, and the United Nations Assembly to implement values for justice, peace, and "limitedness," a humble recognition of our mutual need to share skills and the Spirit's direction.

Social Sin Needs Social Healing

We've been looking at teams operating at the inter-face among society's structures by challenging a key-structure, the formal value-carrier of our culture, EDUCATION. Discarding outmoded forms of education: stereotyped lectures, captive classroom-formations, gift-suppressing approaches to creativity, was the beginning of the change teams could call for to release imagination, gifts, and energies into the culture.

We saw electronic media, especially TV, as most powerful tools for value-change and structure challenge to end the monopoly of a "Reserved Knowledge" through a curriculum of gradually content-enriched "life-studies" for sharing in community.

By "education" I mean the total field of the learning-means available to us including input from "Experience" and "Environment," with "Culture" also conditioning us through all the media. We noted that some structures made up of us befuddled people had lost sight of their goals. When SURVIVAL, then, became our goal, our theology went awry, for our goal suddenly became an *idol:* our poor little tin-pot selves—better still: our poor little chipped-edge pots! When a whole institution goes that way, we have *social sin,* which calls for the healing called change of hearts. Is there a social structure to address social sin? A team?

Law, medicine, government, business, church—any structure, of course, will grow its share of barnacles, but we get to the point where we could lose the ship! When structures become more and more obviously characterized by certain kinds of activity, the demonic can pollute the air, for a structure can *fail to serve love*, so it:

1. stifles human freedom (fails to respond in TRUTH);
2. demeans human dignity (fails to respond in LOVE);
3. promotes human inequality (fails to respond in JUSTICE).

This sick, sick condition calls for healing. But, when the disease is far advanced, we need people who band together to be taught by the Spirit (through their common listening) *what kinds* of solutions are needed for that healing. In a society moving toward greater freedom, toward equalization, such structures need to learn how ineffective they are for today's human person who does not want to be controlled by manipulation or demeaned. Teams could supply the voice needed to speak to and influence structures.

Church and Team: Healing Needed

Is there a stifling of human freedom (failure to respond to truth that makes us free) in church structures at this time? Sociologically, some churches are class-societies: one level of the body claiming rights it denies to others: the have's and the have-not's of privilege, power, office. Down the centuries it has come to this unfortunate division: ordained and not ordained, clergy and laity, trained and untrained, and never the twain shall meet.

The deaconate movement, for Catholics, is part of the effort of Vatican II to restructure, basing the ministries of Christians on the Word, while Anglicans strive to base the theology of the episcopate on mission. Yet churches, in general, remain heavily male-dominated class-societies. The clergy *do* constitute a caste, and the laity, their object of ministry, are without specific rights of their own. Nor do they seem to be considered for promotion to ecclesiastical positions of decision-making, rank, or power. Again, the bishops only, in union with the Pope, can *decide* and *lead*. Sad to say, this structure seems ineffective in reaching people today who want to be represented and make decisions in the bodies of which they are a part.

Furthermore we cannot identify the hierarchical structure of the Church today with the communities of the New Testament.[44]

In fact it is theologically an indefensible position. Hierarchical structure rests on the facts of social history and not in divinely given office. In short, the Church as now constituted at the end of a long evolution is unfortunately an unequal society in terms of competence and rights. Such a structure needs intelligent, loving members (in teams) to bring the Church back into the world by listening creatively to the Spirit's guidance as to HOW to achieve that goal, and by uniting to bring about the changes the Spirit calls for.

"To be a human being is our proper and uniquely inalienable dignity; the highest title of nobility granted us by God."[45] Then why the diminishing of one another sometimes found among the ordained and the nonordained? In regard to service and function, we certainly must respect difference, but not in equality of access to the gifts of the Spirit and Her call to serve the community.

Certain customs, the aura surrounding the Pope: *seda gestatoria*, thrones, tiaras, titles of magnificence borrowed from emperors and monarchs, the sacralization of "priest," his marking with indelible seals—isn't all this a setting-apart and "divinizing" that has no basis in fact? Doesn't it create a regrettable chasm between clergy and laity? Bishops are not made of special clay, nor popes, nor priests, so why not admit the paucity of theological and biblical evidence for claiming anything else? Why not press on to healing the wounds caused by such unfortunate history and theology?

How Heal the Healer?

Other structures, like IBM or General Motors, may have growing pains, but they've been around a day-or-so compared to the 2000-year-old structure of the institutional Christian Church. Yet, fortunately, the healing of church as social form, *its* change of heart, is fundamentally theological. It must, as ever, respond in truth to the Gospel call to this same human freedom, dignity, and equality before God of which we speak.

Recall: *Faith-Stance #2:* We, as Church, wish to be *obedient-to the Spirit* as to *how, when, to whom* gifts are given for the common good.

Aren't we saying again that God *alone* is Sovereign in our

lives? That Jesus is *the* Mediator, and that all of us share in His ministry, His life, through Baptism and through His continuing life in us, the Spirit, in our gifts, calls, empowering with love? Isn't this our dignity, equality, highest freedom?

That's why I suggested above discarding the term "priest," (not necessarily the *function,* once clarified) for a century or so because at *this* time in our history the Spirit calls us to *prove* the truth of our conversion *not* by power and office but by:

SHARING:

I	II	III
Depending on God in *FAITH*	Depending on God in *TRUST*	Depending on God in *LOVE*
FREEDOM from fear so:	FREEDOM from fear so:	FREEDOM from fear so:
Power to *SHARE GOODS*	Power to *SHARE VALUES*	Power to *SHARE FEELINGS*
Serving the Poor	*Teaching and Prophecy*	*Prayer and Worship*[46]

This model of signs of conversion seen in concrete action toward the neighbor doesn't necessarily require a "priested" church, but it *does* need a circular model in which this sharing can happen. How can *gifts, knowledge,* and *power* be shared (dispersed) through the community if the pyramid prevails? Especially, as Outler says, if the people at the bottom of the pyramid are getting all the weight?[47]

Just as teams above called for dispersion of RESERVED KNOWLEDGE and a filtering down of profit and power SHARED in the corporation, so also, the Church as structure will need to study and reform its present allocation of power (inequity) and its development of persons (gifts for sharing).

Why does it need reform? Because "priesthood" and "episcopate" at the moment may be anachronisms and monopolies that perpetuate the inequity, functionally almost inoperative (witness the men who struggle to turn them into life-roles). And they may even become cultic idols. Jesus did not institute either bishops or priests.[48] He gave us His Spirit, *agape*, Love. Everything in the Church is for the service of that message: organization, belief-system, forms, and rites.

And He was severe about inequality: "The kings of the Gentiles exercise lordship over them; and those in authority over them are called benefactors. BUT NOT SO WITH YOU; rather let the greatest among you become as the youngest, and the LEADER AS ONE WHO SERVES (Lk. 22:25-47). Jesus was a lay minister to His brothers and sisters (Lk. 4:16-17), meeting the criteria for the rabbinate: service and preaching of the Word.

Jesus: Not Anti-Liturgical, Not Anti-Priestly

Jesus lived in a time when change, challenge, crisis, produced creativity. He, Himself, affirmed the primacy of the public ministry over cultic priesthood. But this ministry of His WAS an "ordained" service, "selected" to show mercy, strive for justice, and to help the poor. The community proclaimed such a person their "rabbi," when he proved the role by his living it out each day. Jesus Himself took on that role and lived it publicly, apart from the Jewish priesthood and the temple.[49]

Part of our problem today is our having given up Jesus' approach to ministry. Reviving this stance would allow for teams of w&men not only to minister, but, possibly, to be "selected" or publicly ordained for responding to human suffering and injustice according to their gifts. Of course, this implies the ordaining of married couples as well. This would be another possible "way to go" to fit service to human need and not the imposing of institutional forms on a community because "we've always done it that way." If we knew our history, we'd know that's just not so.

What we see now and will see more of will be a healthy proliferation of ministries by everyone, both in variety and diversity, reversing the fourth-century trend to telescope them into the priestly role. But since ministries have to do with established forms of service within a community called "church," this same church (the people in whom the faith of the church resides) should have a vital part in calling forth, accepting, and discerning the special gifts of each member.

This community called church has for its three-fold goal *shar-*

ing the task of proclaiming the good news of Jesus; *being* an example of that proclamation in action (becoming a community of faith, hope, and love) through sharing their lives; finally, they try to spread that good news through service in the real world, the political, social, cultural mix of our everyday lives.

Yet these powers are not personal possessions, but are directly for the service of the community to build up the church:

> . . . his gifts were that some should be apostles, some prophets, some evangelists, some pastors and teachers, for the equipment of the saints, for the work of ministry, for the building up of the body of Christ . . . so that we may no longer be children tossed to and fro and carried with every wind of doctrine . . . rather, speaking the truth in love, we are to grow up in every way into him who is the head, into Christ . . . (Eph. 4:11).

History can save us, too, from repeating the mistakes of our co-religionists separated from us some 400 years. Today in many Protestant groups in the United States the congregation is totally in charge and the clergy often a captive element under their dominance. Some of these ministers can be fired if they oppose too strongly the operative value system of that group, even when they (the clergy) are proclaiming the Gospel.

Catholics complain that they have *no* control over their polity or their pulpits. A dialogue is surely in order, then, for we have no desire to reinvent the wheel when information is there for us. We want to learn from one another's mistakes.

Yet in the case of both groups, I am overcome by the enormous importance not only of the need for gifts discerned by a community, a factor now absent for Catholics, but also the need for every member who exercises a gift to be educated, to have access to "continuous" education. All Christians need access to biblical tradition (Sharing of Scripture below), historical theology: the story of the development of sacramental teaching and practice, to the rich heritage of Christian mysticism and prayer, to all their scriptural, theological, historical heritage.

How can people, "church," congregation, *do* the discerning, deciding, sharing, accepting, understanding, that the concept of co-responsibility calls for without training and education that goes on continually? This continuous education seems to me to be the greatest present priority in the Church. To see to it that the have-not's of knowledge and education, the laity, come into their heritage, now the sole preserve of clergy, sisters, deacons, and professional church people.

We, too, as professionals, may be keeping RESERVED KNOWLEDGE to ourselves. Discerning our talents, understanding our relationships theologically, finding our place in community, allowing other people to breathe as they need to—all these things imply a *continuous education* and I submit that the religious orders of men and women in the United States have a responsibility to help provide it for the laity now. Why not reassess our use of land, money, personnel, and resources and use them for this endeavor: removing the imbalance that makes the Church sick and stifles God's activity in our brothers and sisters because we are the "religious-knowledge" misers of our community world.

Keeping the Power Dispersed

In the early Church the "apostle" always took precedence over the resident "priests and bishops," whom they appointed over churches when they pushed on to the frontier (Eph. 4:11-13). But possession became ten-tenths of the law and the residents, priests and bishops, gradually dominated the missionary thrust. We still have that problem: how to get the Gospel proclaimed in a structured, hierarchical world (for where two or three are gathered together, there *will* be structure) and in differing cultures and political milieux?

How to keep gifts and serving from being co-opted into entrenched powers? No sociological group has ever escaped historically from the eternal vigilance needed as their inspiration gradually became institutionalized. But we, with more *awareness* of such dynamics, could at least build into our new structures more checks and balances to fight the creeping power-play. Most importantly, couldn't we use a *theological* criterion for the dispersion of power? Such as:

Sharing = the Acid Test

THE KINGS OF THE GENTILES EXERCISE LORDSHIP
OVER THEM: BUT NOT SO WITH YOU; RATHER, LET
THE GREATEST AMONG YOU BECOME AS THE
YOUNGEST, AND THE LEADER AS ONE WHO SERVES.
(Lk. 22:25-27)

It seems to me that here's where gifts, serving, organizations, and society's structures all meet: *Sharing as tool for forming the Christian community*, and as basis for the healing of structural ills we've seen above. We may well become "parish" in that sense: w&men joining together and sharing talent, property, energy, money, knowledge, and power to publicly be and to serve groups involved in business, government, communications media, education, etc. (Acts 2:44).

Note that we here see *sharing* again as the touchstone, the litmus paper, that separates the gifts from the illusions. So also with the sharing of KNOWLEDGE, PROPERTY, AND POWER. Not "Do I possess an office bestowed on me by an official process and structure?" but "Do I SHOW FORTH in my life, as Jesus did in His serving, willingness to let go of goods, time, energy, knowledge, and authority (decision-making) for the sake of building community, of BUILDING PEOPLE? The glory of the servant is growing the gifts of others.

Most impractical? Not really, if we apply it to a few examples. And in all of these areas I see teams of w&men operating across national, religious, and racial lines at different levels of competence and operation in good subsidiarity. For instance, applying the principle of the SHARING OF PROPERTY to our major world problem: hunger and the development of peoples. Senator Mark Hatfield says it this way (and he's searching for an "economics to sustain humanity" and not *primarily* a moral stance):

> It is hard to envision successful development in the poor
> nations of the world if comprehensive land reform and in-
> come redistribution are not made the first tasks.[50]

How does "comprehensive land reform and income redistribution" come about in a society often geared to the good of profit and profit alone? Perhaps by letting go our greed. But how? He continues:

> What will be required is what has always been most dif-
> ficult to accomplish without violence: *a redistribution of*

> power and the wealth that brings power; an end to pre-
> emption of resources by the rich; and a replacement for
> the kind of economics that divides the world into con-
> sumers and expendable workers for the sake of acquiring
> more money.[51]

Hatfield acknowledges that he's asking for a revolution, a
spiritual one

> as great as led to the advent of Christianity, requiring
> that man who since the Renaissance has been brought up
> to adore himself, *acquire modesty,* and that we learn the
> lesson of all the atrocities we have experienced for thirty
> or forty years.[52]

In the long run, it seems to go back to something about: to
whomsoever much is given of them much shall be required. The
United States has never known invasion of its homeland, or want,
or disease. And today we are the food-barons of the world. Hatfield concludes with a suggested philosophy: Gandhi's dictum that
"earth provides enough to satisfy every man's need, but not for
every man's greed."

But that implies that we should be converted from our glut-
tony, greed, and pride and turn our energies to serve our neighbor's need, trusting that the Lord will have care of us. What a
field-white for teams, allocating tasks as the Spirit guides: some to
raise public consciousness of the situation, some to work for alternatives, some to lobby, and some to design educational (awareness) tools for schools, TV, radio. Others would work for ecologi-
cal sanity and sharing here and abroad, and all for the redemption
of the earth, our mother, and of our own spirit by sharing the
fruits of the earth with our neighbor.

It is significant that, finally, we begin to understand that ours
is a FINITE planet, not unlimited in resources, not an endless
quarry for exploitation. This fact, plus our spiritual starvation, our
disenchantment with structural oppression, our moving into a tran-
scendental-romantic period—all of these factors help us to understand that we must work together and for one another or perish.
We must turn to the Spirit to change the world as She directs.

These elements are seen in their spiritual manifestation in one phenomenon at least—that of the present Charismatic Movement sweeping through the world, with no stay of national boundary, religion, race, or sex, symbolizing in its powerful freedom the working of the Spirit of Love, Teilhard's "most universal, formidable, and mysterious of cosmic energies."

In the light of our common need, our common fears and yearnings, and the evident power of the Spirit urging us to unity, teams of like-goaled Christians (and all those of good will) can renew the face of the earth: "You shall receive power from on high" (Acts 1:8). Two last "fields-white" suggest themselves among the hundreds ready at hand for teams:

Prisons and Team

One characteristic we have seen above: spiritual blindness and deafness—"eyes that see not; ears that hear not"—caused by turning a deaf ear, closing a blinded-eye to the needs of our neighbor. And the punishment for such obduracy is stone-blindness and deafness because the heart, too, may turn to stone. So, of course, the sharing that follows from awareness of need is impossible because we lack the vitality and energy of the life-giving love of the Spirit in the heart who gives new eyes and ears if we ask, but especially if we listen.

It would be hard to find a field in which this disease operates so effectively as in our corrections-institutions, our prison system. Here our need to ignore, not to know, or to conveniently forget our fellow-citizens' pain operates at a maximum. This often demonic system, a total anomaly in a so-called enlightened society, is the responsibility of the churches (us) who profess to follow the command to ransom the captive given in Jesus' inaugural address at Capharnaum (Lk. 4).

What an area for teams! On every level, in every way, the public must be informed, educated, sensitized. Media must be used, communications networks employed to cry havoc about this open sore in our body politic. Dividing up the work among like-goaled-and-called persons will make it work, alloting tasks according to abilities for lobbying, education, media, visiting, helping prisoners' families.

Above all, we need to practice forgiveness and reconciliation by welcoming back released persons to the community by giving them *jobs*. The lack of jobs is the real reason for the rate of recidivism in the United States, and the lack of jobs may come from our unforgiving hearts. WE are the ones who make any prison sentence a life-sentence if we will not forget, and our frozen hearts ensure that the offender will not be healed, yet we expect forgiveness from the same Father who reads all our hearts.

Local groups exist in each community that can be contacted for information, education, visiting, and writing procedures. Most importantly, teams are needed to study the *long-range aspects* of the problem (and its scandal): abolition of an archaic system, the implementation of creative alternatives, the change of categories for crime—e.g., a bad check sends a man to prison but drunken driving (potential manslaughter) calls for only a fine. By whose reckoning? The protection of property is what it's called. Our society exists to make money so protecting it is often the task of our system of law, justice, and corrections.

Where does the human person's development and the dispersion of power come into that picture? Help needed from the value-system taught by Jesus: "I was in prison and you visited me." Today it would be: "I was gassed, beaten, raped, maimed, and you burnt down the prison with the flame of love: researching, reading, studying, lobbying, writing, using media, investigating; I was in prison and you organized a team."[53]

Teams could ensure, as informed citizens who own the prisons, that we all have:

> (1) ACCESS, through Ombudspersons (not paid by the system) or Citizens'-Committee representatives, to city, county, state, and federal facilities to ascertain conditions, care, and treatment of our fellow-citizens therein.
>
> (2) DECISION-MAKING POWER as Citizens'-Committees (TEAMS) as to the BUILD-ING of prisons in local, state, and federal systems. Why? Where? When? Why not spend the money on *alternatives* that have a chance to work?

(3) OPEN COMMUNICATION between prisoners, press, families, friends and the system that thrives on ignorance and the apathy that follows from it.

(4) A COMPLETE YEARLY AUDITING OF HOW, WHERE, *money* is made and spent IN and BY the prison system, one of the least accountable (financially and otherwise) structures in our society.

> (Goals of the Criminal Justice
> Committee of the "Berkeley Dream"
> Citizens Group)

Teams working on every level would save society the crushing burden of the cost of these truly stupid, ineffective "poorhouses of the twentieth century." They would surely earn the "Come ye blessed of my Father: I was in prison—and you got it on TV, you wrote your Congressman; you exposed custodial brutality, you gave me a job; enter thou into the joy of my Father."

Aging and Teams

If we confine our fellow-human beings to cages called prisons, we also confine others to psychological cells called age-categories. "Past sixty-five is not alive" might be the rallying cry of our production-oriented, profit-driven, dehumanized culture. So when time ripens the human person, again we neither see nor hear; we merely thrust aside and ignore. "Gray" helps make invisible those we never have used our intelligence, imagination, or creativity to educate for aging—from the first-grade on. Better still from the day of birth—to respect life, to cherish it, to use it, and to see its waning as ecologically healthy, natural, and certainly not disastrous.

Teams could function here, as in the prison system, in a great untrodden terrain: social consciousness and social action are needed at every step on the road. *Time* carried a cover-story on some progress made in the field (May 2, 1975), but the public generally remains in ignorance, again, about a vital area of human development left untouched by our educational system, by our media, our communications, and by our social system in general.

Louis J. Putz of Notre Dame, founder and executive director of Harvest House in South Bend, Indiana, has all his life kept his ears, eyes (and heart) open to look beneath surface-need to deepest human need—and moved quickly with organizational skills, Spirit-filled energy and love to provide creative answers to social questions.

He sees the senior citizen as a reservoir of talent, responsibility, experience, and wisdom. The Gray Panthers are an example of the power resident in this group, as well. Note how they are using the CCORRP methodology, along with their charisms, to apply imagination and brains to the role of the aged—and the aging (us) in society. But teamwork, again, is of the essence in this field: contact with local, state, national governments; housing authorities, transportation systems, food and clothing facilities, recreational and entertainment resources—all of these need the working together of dedicated groups. No one can lift *this* monster alone.

Fr. Putz, however, insists that the aging need much more than entertainment or killing time. Retired people are not retarded. Older is not a bad word. Gray is beautiful, too, but chiefly—and here goes imagination and using the Spirit's gifts: older people *must help themselves* as well. They, too, need challenges and growing to make life meaningful. So Harvest House, as one example, is "for the aging, by the aging, and of the aging, a chance to continue learning, developing, harvesting: using hidden talents, learning new skills, having time to HELP OTHERS."[54]

Harvest House people reach out to the hospital, the nursing home, the destitute, through money, counsel, care, companionship. They fight the tendency to die and remain unburied imposed by our insensate society through a six-point program:

> (1) Social Awareness: helping anyone in the area who needs friendship or sociability;
>
> (2) Service: reaching out to one another and all in need, young couples, students, mothers, etc.;
>
> (3) Religious Experience: spiritual development, education for facing aging and death, cre-

ative retreats, spiritual direction, prayer groups, Bible study;

(4) Education and Culture: growing in appreciation of life's beauty, developing talents and skills, sharing them;

(5) Recreation and Celebration: not just passive viewing, but lectures, arts, crafts, dancing, anniversary celebrations, etc.;

(6) Political Power: (nearing twenty million) using voting power, prestige, position, contacts to change discrimination, prisons, facilities for senior citizens, local and state legislation, etc.

What Putz hath put together, let us not hesitate to follow, and like Augustine, be not ashamed that we need to follow—only ashamed not to care, and so to work for ever more creative alternatives to the problems of those sharing the mystery of life with us from the "western chamber" where the view is long, and the color, rose.

A.D.H. = *Alliance for Displaced Homemakers*

The reason why I chose "aging" rather than "aged" for a field-white for teams becomes clear when we look at the work of Tish Sommers and Laurie Shields of Oakland, California. Through the use of skills and teamwork, these two women have already pushed a bill through the California Legislature: The Displaced Homemakers Act (SB 825) to prove that the women over 35—widowed, separated, divorced, job-needy—can recycle skills for needed social services—jobs to use their rich life-experience. Most of all, through the team concept they realize and are teaching others to realize how much they can help one another in this difficult period of transition from dependency to self-sufficiency for women.[55]

Imagine how women, both in that age-group and out of it, with Christian values, could form coalitions and together use this woman-power to address the issues we've seen above: poverty, peace, education, corporate responsibility, etc., which leads us to:

Teams and Sharing the Scriptures

Addressing social evil, challenging the demonic structures,

prophesying (speaking out for God), is a risky business. How can the team, how can the individual member, stay fairly honest? Especially, how avoid all over again a "cliff-stance": us good-guys (up *here*) preaching righteousness to the hard-hearted moneyed moguls (down *there*)?

My fellow-team-members, Clarence and Edee Roberts, felt this urge to serve, to challenge, to change. Part of the growth of their marriage came from that very incentive. Yet they knew soon that they needed more: how to hear God speaking to them, relating to them, through friends, events, through the liturgical community? How to *grow* in an ever-deeper relationship with the Spirit in awareness of self, tendency to judge others, kindness and acceptance?

Their response found in the use of Scripture is described in *Sharing of Scripture (SOS)* soon to be published for use by teams in parish, home, discussion group, liturgical community, etc.[56]

Their goal became and remains to offer each person a chance to grow and develop the gifts of the Spirit through a closer relationship with Christ as they find Him in God's Word. They experienced this contact, relationship, guidance in their own reading and sharing, and that joy pushed them on to share with others. The Spirit did them so move.

Teams: Seed-Bed for Christian Communities

What I suggest is that no matter which field of operation the Spirit moves a group to address, once a team comes together in prayerful goal-setting, let's take most seriously the role of the Word in our work.

This is not just an ad for Sharing of Scripture groups. But it is suggesting strongly that social action not grounded in study and sharing of Gospel-values found in Jesus will be only sounding brass and tinkling cymbal, and not that sounding-SYMBOL: living faith translated into putting on the way-to-live of Jesus, empowered by the Spirit.

And, of course, not only for our own team, but also for all those we meet: to encourage them to study Scripture so that values are grounded, discerned, discussed, prayed through. This ensures that the Spirit remains the leader of each team as She founds Christian community. For authentic Spirit-led teams will lead to the establishment of Christian community. That's why it is so important that we insist that the team membership be *open*.

Open in which way? Open to nonordained, nonclerical, nonofficial church people. Why are most Christian teams made up exclusively of ministers, deacons, sisters, priests? When questioned, these teams point out how much easier it is to work with trained persons, or they argue for the small size of the group as effective for getting the job done. True, but also a trap: more monopoly, more reserved knowledge, less sharing of ideas, goods, self with others, more clericalism, and not the seed-bed for forming a community.

A recent study of team ministry in Hartford, Connecticut, (priests only on the team) revealed some interesting attitudes that still operate strongly in both Catholic and Protestant team service. We find an emphasis on the sharing of authority *among the priests* treated as a concept quite different from the traditional parish set-up, as a result of findings from a sociological study by Douglas T. Hall and Benjamin Schneider of the priests of that diocese. This study found that "the pastor-curate relationship as we have known it should therefore be abolished since it is sociologically, psychologically, and pastorally unsound."

The Hartford Study of Team Ministry which followed these findings was conducted by the Center for Applied Research in the Apostolate (CARA) of Washington, D.C. Their researchers found that "team ministries (priests only) are not more effective than other ministries as they exist in the (Hartford) archdiocese today. But it can be said that they are effective."

What struck me both in the findings and in the language of the study is the use of the term "team ministry" in such a limited sense without a "louder" statement of its exclusiveness. Throughout my text, I apply that designation, "team," only to those groupings of women and men (ordained and not ordained), single or married, who together *represent* in some authentic fashion (e.g., election) the people they wish to serve, a telling prerequisite absent in the Hartford model. Expressions such as the following were most striking to me:

. . . While in many senses team ministry was introduced chiefly *in order to promote the priests' personal growth*, the people who were to be served were ever-present as the ultimate *beneficiaries at whom* the changes were directed.

The people to be served are not "beneficiaries" in the model I envision, nor are changes directed *at* them. Through CCORRP, especially through Representation and Participation (in decision-making), they are Part of the team through sharing their gifts, giving and receiving from and *with* the ordained/professional members.

It's hard to see, then, how a team can function without representatives of those we intend to serve: the laity, the community. This is such a simple principle, but just watch how often it's not observed. Then teams wonder why they fail, why they don't seem to be in touch with the local community or know its problems. Most harmful, however, is the bad theology operating. Nonordained folks *do* have gifts for community. Our "men's club," "women's club," idea of teams, especially *ordained-only* types, can become an exclusive in-group and offer little help in involving a total community in areas of service.

For this reason sharing of Scripture is essential, along with prayer and worship, if we're to keep our heads on straight about who we are and what we're about, if we're to stay open to the Spirit's powerful messages through our members. If teams do get too large, and after we get to eight members that's a real possibility, just form another team, supply another area, follow the leading of the Spirit. If we stay open through prayerful discernment, there's no telling what, where, when, and to whom the Spirit will bid us go. And that's the whole idea: "the word of the Lord increased." This is the criterion for the true progress of the group, of their mission, their service (Acts 6:7; 12:24; 19:20).[57] It is this spreading of the word of God that the Spirit uses to make us one, and so re-found Her "church," the gathered ones, but gathered by the Spirit by whom alone we can say: "Jesus is Lord."

They that wait upon the Lord shall renew
    their strength;
they shall mount up with wings as eagles;
they shall run and not be weary;
they shall walk, and they shall not grow faint (Isaiah
    40:31).

VII. TEAM TECHNOLOGY—
THE PRACTICE OF "TEAM"
—THE "HOW" OF
ENABLING CHANGE

All the charismatic gifts have to do with how, *concretely,
human beings are enabled to cope with the multiple and
variegated claims of death. The charismatic gifts furnish
the only powers to which humans have access against the
aggressions of the principalities. These gifts dispel idola-
try and free human beings to celebrate Creation, which is
. . . integral to the worship of God. The gifts equip us to
live humanly in the midst of the Fall. The exercise of
these gifts constitutes the essential tactics of resistance to
the power of death (William Stringfellow).*

Christ came to set us free to love. He said: "Love as I have
loved you" (Jn. 15:12). So the serving of Jesus is our model for
loving and serving.

Jesus trained His apostles and set them free through giving
them *power and responsibility* to proclaim the good news that all
of us are loved by God. Which means we, too, are involved in
calling for the change of heart that leads to the forgiveness of
alienation and refusal-to-grow when we serve like Him. Jesus set
up the model for that conversion-process in His "Desert Experience" when He parried the temptations that beset every loving
server.

Jesus was finally executed in the tension between the "IS" of
His society and the "OUGHT-TO-BE" He called for: *conversion.*
His challenge, so clear, so powerful, so demanding, was supremely

threatening. So He had to die. When we, continuing His ministry, call for change of heart today we need not expect less. We'll just have to die in different ways, perhaps: to human-respect, to pride, to status, to greed, to lust for power, to envy—above all, maybe, to achieving some cherished *individual* goals.

But the reaction from society will be the same: calling for *real change* produces fear and threatening—even fear and trembling. If we are agents of reconciliation (2 Cor. 5:18), friend-makers, then before the mending of fences or the repairing of broken relationships can take place, hearts must open to change.

Our own hearts have tried to respond to God's lavishly given love by a life of loving and serving others. Power to change, like prayer, is a theological grace, not a psychological feat, so we make prayer for those-we-serve part of the tissue of our serving, waiting on the Lord for the moment of His turning toward us all in mercy, asking Him to be the heart-opener.

While we wait, pray, and work for change in society, still we're *involved* in it. We're a large "group," running on the laws of sociology and the dynamics of groups (forces operating in a group). So, social science must complement our theological-spiritual serving with professional know-how about groups, society's and ours!

That means not only knowing about but *practicing* group dynamics, what we'll call the Technology of Groups. Our previous formula operates here, too:

$$PROBLEM > ISSUE > NEED > GOAL = \begin{cases} CALL & = STRATEGY + TACTICS \\ & (PLAN) & (STEPS \\ FOR & & IN\ PLAN) \\ CHANGE & = THE\ "HOW"\ OF\ CHANGE \end{cases}$$

In order to change ourselves as individuals or as team, to change society, we'll need good psychology, sociology, theology, spirituality, and at the nitty-gritty level good group technology: the *practice* of group dynamics and group skills. All of them involving a change in *attitudes* (See Behavior Circle: See-Level) if we want to change behavior.

The change of heart, leading to the change of behavior, is the goal of our ministry, of our serving each other as Christians, as fellow-citizens. CHANGE is the Fourth Human Basic, the normal human condition. It is the serving situation (life-situation) of dying and rising with Jesus now.

To bring it about, we marshal all knowledge and power available, all skills, all tools. Once we accept the fact that change is normative for our serving, we can get to work learning how to use it through this Team Technology.

Some HOW'S for ACHIEVING CHANGE

Model I   To help bring about change *in our* Team AS TEAM, so our team becomes:

A TARGET OF CHANGE

Model II   To help bring about change through pressures from the team itself on its OWN MEMBERS, so the team becomes:

A MEANS OF CHANGE

Model III   To turn the organized efforts of our team towards affecting change *OUTSIDE* our own group, so the team becomes:

AN AGENT OF CHANGE

Since I assume, from our theology of serving above, that teams are primarily *agents of change/reconciliation* by their share in Jesus' ministry (proclaiming God's love and asking for conversion of heart), we probably agree that Model III is our ordinary operating common change-form. So let's concentrate first on the two vehicles for change above: team as *target*, and team as *means* of change. Then we'll see ourselves as *agents*.

MODEL I. OUR TEAM AS A TARGET OF CHANGE[32]

What are we doing here? Two things: (1) we're looking at our own operation, examining performance, organization, cohesion, communications, etc. So we're diagnosing our team's *condition*;

(2) we're looking at a *suggested* procedure for use in regular quarterly *team-evaluations* we may need to use. We're killing two birds.

We're also using the Third Human Basic, Social Feedback, to help us bring about the Fourth: Change, and in an organized, measurable procedure. So this model can be used to see why we're not operating well or *how* we're operating through a regular Check-Up procedure (frequently agreed upon by the team).

Many teams bring outside facilitators/consultants in to help do this analyzing and feedback. A very good idea, since the psychology of the team often forbids our own members doing a self-evaluation of this nature. Using the "outsider" frees team members to respond more easily.

Perhaps advanced teams can use their own resource-members to do this check-up-analysis, but new teams might find it difficult to get distance and neutrality enough to be honest about where they are—when they're only six months on the road to finding out!

When the team itself is the target of change, we're making the basic assumption that to get the team to change *as team*, we'll have to agree on the NEED for change. So we need to agree on *how we see* that need in relationship to our goals.

Then we get some steam, some motivation to do the job of changing ourselves: our own conversion-experience.

This is not easy if the needed change found through prayer, analysis, social feedback, honest communication and careful procedure turns out to be dropping a member from the team. Or adding a new one. Or deciding this team should terminate its operation! Or change its primary goal!

Once we're agreed on the NEED for change, we can run through the checklist (Section V) of essentials for team ministry, breaking them down under the following headings:

A. ANALYZING OUR ORGANIZATION

1. 1. *Goals*

    (a) Are we still agreed on these? Why/Why not?
    (b) If we want to change them, HOW?
    (c) Are we facing up to conflict between individual, personal goals and team goals?

(d) If we're not agreed on goals, HOW are we settling this? Will we keep it a group decision?

2. *Objectives*

(a) Are these action steps clear, realistic, designed to move us step-by-step to our goal in the light of resources: people, time-line, energy, structure? Are they measurable?

(b) Do we HAVE target dates, a time-line?

(c) Who is responsible for which objectives and do they give regular feedback on accomplishment of these to the team?

3. *Structure*

(a) *Power Structure:* Who decides about goals, objectives, work allocation?

(b) How is your shared decision-making working? Is it OVERworked? Is democracy so rampant we don't have time to work—or pray?

(c) *Choice-Structure:* Who likes/dislikes whom? Do they face up to it and ventilate it? Will it jeopardize the goals of the team? How can it be used positively?

(d) *Role-Structure:* Do people's roles really follow from their talents and gifts? Who is getting un-roled, and by what/whom?

(e) *Communication-Structure:* (see above) NEVER skip this part of your Team X-ray: "of the essence"!

(f) *Reward Structure:* Is the Love-Road and the Love Means really operating on our team (See above, p. 60). Are the Spirit's gifts in one another being acknowledged and shared? Is jealousy a problem?

B. GAUGING OUR PRESSURE in regards to Norms and Standards (Social Pressure):

(1) Difference (See-Level) respected, rather than Conformity awarded?

(2) Are Dependence and Independence kept in fairly good balance?

(3) Whose Expectations are pushing whom/what? Whose ambitions are doing same? Do we think that's good or not, and why?

(4) Is the tone: "We've always done it this way!" or is there a chance for: "Let's give this a try." (See "Killers" below, p. 134).

(5) How do we resolve differences of opinion or relationship? By what sort of pressure?

(6) What's the attitude of the Team toward those who are *non-Team*? (Quite crucial; in fact, it's litmus paper to test the Christian quality of our team: there must be no stranger! Is out-reach growing?)

(7) Whose personal influence is creating pressure? Is that good/not?

Note Well: We're trying to keep a balance in the delicate matter of *Team See-Level* influencing *Individual See-Levels*, so we have to watch:

(a) fostering human growth in persons;

(b) fostering achievement by the team;

(c) resisting too-strong personalities so that they may not coerce others, while building "quieter" types;

(d) striving for organizational structure, use of leadership, talents, and good dynamics: *technology and tact.*

C. MEASURING OUR COHESION: Are we growing in wisdom and grace?
Are we growing in acceptance of one another?

SIGNS OF GROWTH

(1) *Phases in the GROWTH of the Team:* Check-See:

(a) Are procedures and methods evolving, self-correcting? In process?

(b) Are we using problem-solving, conflict-resolution? regular feedback sessions, like this one? how? how often?

(c) Feelings: Where do we see growth in openness, ventilation, freedom from fear and intolerance? What are we doing with disenchantment, disappointment, flight or fright? Do we make sure that fear and anger can be expressed? By what mechanisms?

(d) Are our gifts used in our roles attaining goals: are we what we want to be to enable others to grow *their* gifts? Is this a "growing" thing? (*pace!*)

(2) *Some Stages in Team Cohesion:*

(a) *The Personal Reference Stage:* we're concerned with our personal goals and problem: hidden agendas, the ordinary human condition of any team.

(b) *Dissatisfaction Stage:* Honeymoon officially over! Our urge to give of ourselves is pulled back by protecting our personal goals, by an often unconscious fear of letting go to team goals.

(c) *Insight Level:* through honest communication, expression of feeling, especially anger, shared responsibility, influence, etc. We begin to feel PART of the team. We see the Common Vision.

(d) *Decision:* We work through the Stay/Go Syndrome; make up our minds about the cost of either road, and finally make a choice.

(e) *Satisfaction Level:* Experiencing teamwork, belonging, common prayer, goals, viewpoints, and use of our time, energy, self, love.

Now, if as team we've found *we* need to change, let's get the information out to the total group, get feedback from everyone, ask for plans and ideas from each member and possible results they see coming from the proposed changes.

Notice that this will mean *communicating.* Bet you anything that if there's a trouble-spot on the team, it will show up in this area. Once the team-process of evaluating gets feedback *out loud* and *from everybody*, some barriers to communication built up brick-by-brick may fall.

Don't be afraid of the falling bricks. Sometimes they even get tossed—and at people! That's great, for honest expression of real disagreement IS communication: one form of it. Communication means that meanings meet, so if we disagree, we need honestly to say so. Teamwork and routine may have buried that need for quiet or shy members. Yet, the feeling and the disagreement (their roots) are real and will have to be ventilated if working together joyfully is to happen.

Planning Change

Remember that planning change involves people, people who, in general, are threatened by change. Especially if you plan to change a team procedure, method, function, goal. See-Levels will get stepped on, so, first:
(1) Examine the assumptions and the expectations, the fears of each team member frankly.
(2) Share together how the change will affect each member's role, power-place, schedule, relationships.
(3) Relate the change to team values and to individual values that have become our goals.

Never forget: Change implies helping people to develop fitting behavior (if there's to be a *new* setting, situation, role), to keep on being imaginative, effective, loving.

Reducing Resistance

This means good working-together as team to *reduce resistance* (all of us) to the needed change:
(1) Be sure everybody has complete, accurate information.
(2) Present a clear picture of the desired change.
(3) Involve each member of the team in PLANNING the change.
(4) Always take individual See-Levels into account; don't tread on them!
(5) Help to reduce *fear of changes in interpersonal relationships* because of the change.

Producing Change

Notice that the *prime movers for change*, always deeply ticking, are among the following:

(1) personal affirmation of the self in some way;

(2) fear of loss of some role or relationship;
(3) love or affection gained or lost;
(4) conformity to group-pressure;
(5) inspiration and example of others;
(6) discontent over unsatisfied need;
(7) deep motivations like love, joy, fear, zeal.

Even so, we will still have some deep-seated resistance to change, especially in a well-established team. For instance, if we add a *new* member, suddenly the status quo stands on end—and for all the reasons we've cited above, because a team is a bundle of relationships and habits.

Yet, if we recall that personal change always begins in that area of "most-control": our *daily* relationships, then we hope that team cohesion can motivate us to make the adjustment in schedule, role, task, etc. Communication can smooth the change-process within the team. Just pray somebody can add the spice of humor!

"Killer" Statements that get thrown around a team to stop: growth, creativity, flexibility, imagination, and just plain-ol'-change:

1. We've never done it before.
2. We don't have the time.
3. We've always done it this way.
4. We're not ready for it.
5. The women will never buy it.
6. Our team is different.
7. The team will scream!
8. It's too visionary.
9. We don't have the money.
10. Can't teach an ol' dog new tricks.
11. We're doing OK without it.
12. Send it to a committee.
13. It's too much trouble to change.
14. It won't work on our team.
15. The men won't like it.
16. We don't have the personnel.
17. We'd have to use "lay-people."
18. We can't take the chance.

19. It's not our problem.
20. Why doesn't she have a check-up?

(If you use these for fun in your orientation, it soon gets to be enough just to say the NUMBER of the Killer to get a howl.)

Getting Our Team to Change

Note that calling for change in our team means challenging some VALUES, raising ISSUES in regard to GOALS, PROCE-DURES, and ROLES. As a mini-structure, we are experiencing in microcosm what we hope society will experience through our serving together: the call to change. We, as a team, question some of society's VALUES, PROCEDURES, IMPOSED ROLES. Above all, we begin to experience what it is to try to change VALUES that have frozen into HABITS, even our own.

We begin to realize, too, that a purely technological, sociological, or psychological approach to the process of change is insufficient. These aspects of change are vital as a basis for our understanding of human process and systems, but deeply operative also are the "Powers of this World" (the *exousiai*) and the Fiery Wheel of the Spirit's power in, through, and beyond this world and deep in our hearts. As we analyze and call for change, then, our own praying, fasting, and crying aloud for justice together in worship and work becomes an essential complement to the use of good technology.

We could use value-clarification, values-consciousness, strategies for change, decision-making, conflict-resolution, transactional analysis—shall I go on? They are all useful and we gladly make use of them, pausing always however to listen to and for the Spirit's effortless, powerful in-surging of our team, changing—in the flash of a wing—a human heart, a faltering step, a fearful spirit.

How to pattern *value* into *virtue*, or good habit, our life-task, is such a mysterious amalgam of our sweat-and-tears and the Spirit's loving infusion that we can only rejoice to work at it in a glorious blur of synergic-sharing.

Meanwhile, we do our daily-dozen gladdened by the song in our hearts: we ARE loved, we ARE empowered, we need not FEAR, for She is with us always. In that Spirit, we can use every technical tool and skill to change our own value-system, goals, or operation—or society's.

MODEL II. OUR TEAM AS MEANS OF CHANGE

With hearts thus fortified by love, let's go on to how about changing us? One possible way to look at this is to study how to use our team as a *means of change*, IF the change we want involves getting some of *us* to change so that the *team* can change. After all, we are the team.

If that's the case, then, we need to flash back to Chapter V: the "what" of team serving, to see what elements must be operating so that members of our team can allow themselves freely to change.

Group as Means of Change

(1) A strong WE-feeling (*Sense of Belonging*) must exist if those-to-be-changed and those wanting-change desire their meaning to meet.

(2) *Affection* (loving and being loved) is the pervasive atmosphere of the team. So members will be influenced by the loving-power of the team to be carried forward into desired change. How impossible without prayer!

(3) The desired change must be seen to be closely related to the *goals* of those being affected by the change. Note importance of long series of goal-setting sessions in past where member had a chance freely to embrace the goals or discard them. Now she honestly can distinguish whether the new change fits her goals.

(4) The desired change must, of course, be related to the *needs* of members.

(5) The informal structure of the group can operate in this situation; i.e., the choice-structure (likes and dislikes) of members can help bring about change if those they care for want the change.

(6) Since group pressure to conform can really push members, it's very important to pray with and through the choice of change, and not just let social pressures and human respect shove weaker members into dumb acquies-

cence. The goal is to say "WE" in consensus, for patience and openness are of the essence, and not a tally of votes!

Just the listing of factors needed for the group to become a *means of change* for its own members proves that some people probably *cannot* operate on a team. Their gifts, their talents, or temperaments will not tolerate such a process as that above.

So, that's fine! We do *not* assume that team ministry's the only way to fly. The Spirit is the only way to fly. The form of service for each of us will work out through learning our gifts, through listening to each other and the Spirit. The vehicle for those gifts need not always be a team.

MODEL III: OUR TEAM AS AGENT-OF-CHANGE

The group as *agent*-of-change (producing change in persons and groups *outside* the team) is the subject of another book, not this one. The materials on community organization, social action, and methods of social change exist in abundance and will surely be used by the team as part of their theoretical and practical training.

I prefer to keep to considering the team in itself, seeing it as a small social system of its own in which forces operate so that social change can happen as the Spirit calls the group to action wherever they find human need and the Spirit's call. In the next chapter, however, I will mention some possible future areas of service for the team as an agent-of-change.

To continue our study of the change-enablers: we've seen Group Theory and Practice operating to help us set up a team, to gauge its condition, and to evaluate it periodically. In other words, we've taken a look at some means for making changes through growth in our knowledge and skills.

Deep beneath them in the Behavior-Circle lie our *attitudes.* Changes in attitude are not so easily checked or measured as those in the previous two. This is easily said, but harder to live with. Resistance from attitudes will recur again and again as cause for opposition to any proposed change in the team or its members.

We can never forget that when we call for change we're possibly stepping on somebody's See-Level and threatening thereby their values and attitudes and challenging their behavior. When we've assessed changes in operation, work, roles, information, still let's always check gently for attitudes. They stick harder in the psyche and resist change to the death.

Only changes in the See-Level that truly change values can get to attitudes—the reason why we keep after steady team education, theological reflection, open loving environment, shared experiences to shape us into instruments for change, no matter *whose* chips: our own or our neighbor's!

Leadership

Change can take place, then, through evaluation, through feedback, through motivation of attitudes. But, besides, we can always rely on the uncontrollable X-Factor: the Spirit's delightful giving of gifts for change and conversion in the circle of team, now to one, now to another.

You recall our leadership definition: moving from the *technical*: "Leadership is exercising influence in a group in a given situation through communication" to the *theological*: "Leadership (as sharing) is exercising influence multiplied a thousand-fold by the Spirit in the community through presence and mission."

To keep that insight-filled power-of-the-Spirit (leadership) moving around a group, again, good technology lays out a highway to opening eyes and ears to increase awareness and alertness when the Spirit decides to move. Leadership, like structure, is vital for the tone, the élan, the success of a team. The question remains: which kind?

Plunging into the life-stream of a group as participating members involves risk, fear, uncertainty—above all the fear, perhaps, of *being* changed, even when our very participation says we're willin'! So we need a kind of Mutual-Leadership that can enable that fear out of us and lay our hearts open to the Spirit, especially to Her speaking through each of us to the others.

So the atmosphere of the team is permissive: no fear, no intolerance. People can say what they think and feel: acceptance. Here are some prerequisites for establishing that climate for growing communal-leadership:

(1) Mutual respect for individual opinions; no preaching, no condemnations.

(2) Honest evaluation of one's own feelings and ideas; recognizing those of others.

(3) Free association-discussion allowed for expressing feelings to get person-to-person relationships out loud.

(4) Developmental discussion, i.e., the attempt to solve a problem, always allowed when the group decides.

The shelves are loaded with volumes on leadership. Gordon L. Lippitt, an authority in this field, feels that some basic elements comprise the following *Check-List for Development of Team Leaders:*

1. *Insight into self:* know your own feelings and motivations: to accept ourselves before we can fully accept others.

2. *A modicum of personal security:* so as to be nonpunitive in relating with members, and therefore, able to listen without needing self-justification.

3. Keep your *behavior consistent* with your intentions as an outgrowth of personal security and interpersonal skills.

4. *Appropriate sensitivity* to situations: awake to the formal and informal levels of the session, to where people are: listen to the music (the nonverbal) as well as the ideas presented.

5. *Diagnostic ability:* can you diagnose the *causes*: the emotional and rational needs ticking in the group?

6. *Flexibility* in one's role relationships: not the same as being confused! but the ability to function in different roles to resolve problems and help further action.

7. *Continuous learning:* to learn how to learn: from failures, frustrations, achievements, joy, and sorrow.

Notice how each one of the above qualifications presupposes an openness to the Spirit's helping-power, a loving awareness of the needs of others as friends, a willingness to listen and learn (humility), in other words, growth in the practice of Christian love patterned into virtue. Technology says how to exercise influence. The Spirit reminds us *whose*!

Permissive vs. Directive

Often, studies divide leaders into directive or authoritarian and permissive or nondirective types. A combination of the two seems to work, depending on the given situation. Research has shown that the leadership that develops maturity draws out by careful-questioning to help others clarify their own ideas. Instead of initiating action for others, it often helps them arrive at decisions they've participated in freely and responsibly. This is the permissive leader at her best, expressing self freely, letting others do the same.

I've always enjoyed Karl Rahner's delightful phrase in which he says the real leader doesn't imitate an "Olympian Papa"—I add: "nor Mama"!—but recognizes the common fallibility of all of us.

How about the authoritarian/directive leader? This person has a way of making others feel dependent on her, even passive and inferior. She is not too interested in developing a sense of responsibility in team members unless it helps accomplish *her* personal goals.

This type of leadership creates an atmosphere of rivalry, a consequent lack of cooperation and trust. It even produces hostility among the competitors, exactly what team members may be manipulated to become.

The consequent frustration under this style of leadership leads to a decrease in individual efficiency, especially among the more mature members who find even some kinds of permissive leadership onerous. Why? Because, in general, psychologically healthy people find that they need to develop:

(1) from being passive as an infant to more active as adults;
(2) from being dependent upon others to being relatively independent;
(3) from being a subordinate in a family to achieving an equal or higher status;
(4) from expressing a few opinions to expressing many.[34]

Under permissive leadership it's true that there are fewer frustrations and conflicts since the person has a better chance to develop in healthy fashion. Yet, for the more mature, conflict will often still exist. Why? Probably the structure and organization of the team itself is at fault. A too-formal structure, not permitting opinions about goals or the way to achieve them, can still curb the normal development mature people demand.

> The nearer modern society comes to the state of *total organization*, the more difficult it is to find any place for spiritual freedom and personal responsibility. Education itself becomes an essential part of a machine, for the mind has to be as completely measured . . . as the task which it is being trained to perform.[35]

How to combat it? Try the check-list on "Structure" above adjusting for the goal of free expression, free association, and developmental discussion.

Is the group too large, for instance? Once the team goes over seven or eight key members, we're moving out of the number of possible close relationships for any of us to maintain. Our Lord Jesus had Twelve in His group, but only because He was God!

In any case, *informality* is often the key to over-tight structure. As the group works out its questions on goals, structures, power, it will progress in depth of encounter and dialogue. It will develop an internal unity, produced by the combined efforts of members if they all share this concern (aloud) for mature discussion. The more informal the structure the faster this internal unity will develop, given the prayerful, honest use of diagnosis above.

More important than any other leadership tool is our mutually *respecting each other's different See-Levels.* Recall here my remarks about men's being aware of the need for women to have a chance to express their needs, fears, ideas, feelings.

Yet, can women in the group let men be as myopic as they are about women (we think) and give them a chance to work that through while we hold the line as to who we are—but with patience and loving concern? Both See-Levels are vibrating, and neither can hear the other, unless each tries to listen openly to the Spirit's possible piece of good news: women for men, men for women.

Nothing can be more fruitful and growth-ful than the complementarity of men and women on the team if they will allow themselves to be educated by one another about where they are honestly, seriously, openly, painfully, and delightfully! Some men do have an enormous amount to learn about women's abilities, talents, personhood, ambitions, and just plain gifts.

And women, in general, need to drop some of their stereotypes about men: demanding too much or too little, not being honest, letting fear of ridicule or failure keep them from following the Spirit's call to serve *their* way, and not the way they think men would approve. Otherwise, why bother with a team?

Real leaders, as their turn comes up to coordinate, will be deeply aware of the human potential they can help release if they're only awake, aware of the need to remove roadblocks—which may include knocking away at some blocks in the shape of heads! Leadership can't always be fun!

OUFCA—as we say in Swahili!

Speaking of leadership leads us to a neat, thumbnail mnemonic to mumble to yourself when it's your turn to coordinate: it's pronounced OUFCA. That's right! It goes like this:

O = *OBJECTIVITY:* How do you usually see things? Can you transcend a merely personal view? Can you make decisions without being too much pushed by extraneous factors? Are you fairly impartial?

U = *UNDERSTANDING PEOPLE:* Can you usually say to yourself: "I think I can begin to understand somewhat how she thinks, feels, why she does what she does." Can you give yourself to absorbing something of the mystery of others as life's most interesting task?

F = *FLEXIBILITY:* The real ringer! Most difficult aspect of leadership! Why? Habit, of course; our ideas, assumptions, even our feelings run in carved-out channels. Can you change your plans on short notice? Switch methods? approaches? Can you hang loose, especially when chairing your session? And after?

C = *COMMUNICATIONS-MINDEDNESS:* Handled in depth above (Section V). Do you know how to use ways of getting ideas, feelings across to others . . . to make meaning meet? How do you use words, media? Are you convinced of the power of radio, TV? Nonverbals?

A = *AUTHORITY:* Do you know when to be firm, when to let things go? How do you get this group to go along with what you see as important while respecting their freedom and dignity? What happens to you when you have power? Are you adamant with yourself when you hold power as to receiving *honest, anonymous* feedback about your handling of that radioactive substance? Do you use ordinary tools like anonymous questionnaires, evaluation sheets to get such feedback about your own performance and how you make people feel?

The coordinator works for:

1. KNOWING SELF AND ACCEPTING SELF
2. SOME PERSONAL SECURITY: NOT THREATENED
3. FAIRLY-CONSISTENT BEHAVIOR: DEPENDABILITY
4. SENSITIVITY TO SITUATIONS
5. UNDERSTANDING PEOPLE: READS MUSIC
6. DIAGNOSTIC-BILITY: READS CAUSES
7. OBJECTIVITY: FAIRLY IMPARTIAL
8. COMMUNICATIONS-MINDED: USES MEDIA
9. FLEXIBILITY: NONRIGID THINKER
10. CONTINUOUS LEARNING: GROWER
11. OBEDIENT TO AUTHORITY: LISTENS TO THE SPIRIT IN SELF AND TEAM
12. HUMOR: CAN LAUGH AT SELF'S GAMES AND DECEPTIONS

THE COORDINATOR

Looking back at this section on leadership may help turn more lights on the ever-present question for a team: whom to recruit, what to look for, and how to gauge our own team-performance right now.

Note that we've brought together in the OUFCA mnemonic and in the sections above a galaxy of attributes needed for leading and coordinating, especially if we mean by that coordinating the talents of *others*: the growing of people.

To put it another way, the coordinator is called upon to handle the lived-tension between individual and group attempts to follow the Spirit's call. If a gift involves an ability for exercising a

particular talent in community, that gift implies a facility, an ease
in fulfilling that service, but how, when, where? And what about
the rights of other gifted people?

Still another way to say it: the coordinator is entrusted by the
community with *authority* to facilitate the working-together of
gifts to avoid chaos and to "order" serving with a minimum of
duplication, confusion, and frustration (1 Cor. 2:47).

Each team member who buys our common theology knows
indeed that s(he) must follow a call, but knows, too, that the greatest of all the gifts is LOVE (1 Cor. 13). The charismatic structure
of the Pauline churches was built on that premise: love (*agape*) is
the greatest of these! And the goal of our loving is to build the
group, the *community*, the fellowship. Gifts are for group.

In the light of love as first and highest gift, the reason for all
the others, it's easier to see how *my* gift might not have to function
at *this* precise moment. Another member could see why *his* might
have to be quiescent on *that* project, etc. All *together* turn to the
coordinator-of-the-moment to order this mutual exchange of
dying-to-self and rising-with-the-group. S(he) needs to help facilitate this giving and receiving of gifts, implying sometimes a giving-
up, an emptying-out, painful but ultimately profitable both for individual and team.

This leader-coordinator is chosen by our team, and therefore
executes our *shared decisions* for us, for the fellowship. So her gift,
too, is used for the group, facilitating the ease-full use of the gifts
of the group in harmony.

Once upon a time this was the role of the hierarchical structure: an agent of order in a community alive with charisms, but
with a task to perform: to become what they were, the People of
God. Theirs was a pastoral theology that needed good order to facilitate the practice of that theology in the ministry of Jesus continued through w&men in every time and place.

Must One Person Coordinate?

This practical question will always be around in a period of
anti-authoritarianism. The answer (for me) is YES! Simply because good group dynamics for a serving team, task-oriented as
well as person-centered, calls for some executive-person to implement the team decision-making of the group. Every decision can-

not be made by a group. Too often we would manufacture a camel, for sure! Someone must shoulder the "representative," "public" role for the group.

So, in spite of where our See-Level leaves us on this question, I'd advise electing, choosing, or designating through *team-decision* one person (for a time, also designated) to do executive-coordinating for the team. The person so chosen (and the team) can look to guidelines like those above, especially those questions under "Authority," to evaluate the coordinator's performance.

Motivation: Power for Change

A. *Chief Means Discussed thus far: Summary:*
   1. Team feedback and Evaluation Geared to Change
   2. Individual Gifts of Leaders Moving for Change
   3. Group Gifts of Team Discerning Need for Change
   4. Continuous Development of Know-How and Skills for Change
   5. Built-in, Long-Range Planning for Necessary Change: Accommodation to Changing-Pastoral-Needs
   6. Reducing Resistance to Change: On-Going Process of Meetings, Evaluation, Prayer, and Affectivity

B. *Change-Motivation*

Areas:
   1. Psychological: love, acceptance, joy, fear, ambition
   2. Theological: acceptance of sovereignty of Spirit to give power and gifts to whomever She will, even to *me*!
      acceptance of my individual role on team
      acceptance of roles of others on team as obeying Spirit's authority

Implementation:
   1. How? Through keeping bright the GOAL: if adequate, both *motivation* and *authority* problems will fall into line. Use means above for polishing team-goals.
   2. Watch organizational structure for line and staff, circle-operation of power, decision-making, and responsibility = feeds motivation and zeal.

3. *Means To Effect Procedural Success:*
   a. *Diagnosing:* —Issues that can become problems.
      Relationships that can become problems.
   b. *Leveling:* —Work for communication; against fear.
      —Work for trust, risk, acceptance.
   c. *Communicating:* See above.
   d. *Achieving:* —Help Expectations become operative in Roles that match Gifts
      —Stimulate to further growth through *Love-Road* and *Love-Means* (above, p. 60).
   e. *Affiliating:* —Work together and individually on *Need Satisfiers:*

      Trust
      Acceptance
      Recognition
      Belonging
      Identifying
      Commitment

C. Change for the team, then, comes about, among many other factors, from:
Changes in:
1. ATMOSPHERE: Climate of Acceptance, no fear/intolerance
2. SHARED LEADERSHIP: The Spirit leads the Team through elected members
3. PROCESS: Using proper Dynamics and Skills
4. CONTENT: Goal and Achievement
5. PSYCHIC PRESSURES: (a) Emotional tone
   (b) Energy levels
   (c) Time-pressures

(d) Degree of interest
(e) Degree of attention
(f) Degree of love: the presence and activity of the Spirit fed by the
(g) Degree of prayer, contemplation, reflection, and sharing of feelings, especially *fear* and *anger*.

Above all, I believe authentic change comes about through these last two (f, g), because once I share my fear and even my anger with you I become a real person. You can now identify with me, for you too feel fear and anger, but may often feel that they are socially unacceptable, so you don't express or ventilate them. Then they fester.

Finally, your being "weak" with me, expressing fear and anger just like mine, allows me to *identify* with you, with all team members, and with the Jesus who was afraid in the garden, who prayed for His cup of pain to pass away, who begged His team members to stay and pray with Him (Mt. 26:36-46). The sharing of our humanity can be a most powerful liberator, a true motivation for change, even our own.

People are motivated when they can be shown how to break through a barrier (Need) and achieve a goal. Working successfully with people is far from easy. Understanding people is even more difficult—next to love, we crave understanding the most. The true measure of leadership—at any level of business or professional activity—is the capacity of an individual to be sensitive and understanding of these basic needs in others: . . . the drive for life and self-preservation, to love and be loved, to be appreciated, have self-respect and importance, to develop potential through self-realization of spiritual needs (James Siress, Management Consultant: Lawrence-Leiter & Company).

Group Dynamics Dictionary

DAVID H. JENKINS, PH.D.

Conformity: Often seen as something to be resisted in order to maintain "individuality"; not often clearly seen as the need to work out some agreements and understandings about working together as a group to which all members can conform so the work can be accomplished. Conformity to work procedures helps to get work done; conformity to ideas and the resulting denial of differences and capabilities eliminates the major resources which are needed in order to get work done. Major question is: "In what areas is conformity useful?"

Consensus: Condition in which all members of the group agree to the particular action, decision or control; at best it is a truly felt agreement, without a sense of pressure from others; more easily achieved in a cohesive group. Not ordinarily secured through voting; works most easily when it occurs almost automatically as the group moves ahead. When secured, usually aids the resulting work, as it removes resistance. Requires members to be group-oriented in their behavior.

Dialogue: A discussion (technically two people, but often more) in which the people are attempting to listen to each other and really understand each other (often a new experience). Quite difficult to perform in this culture; represents "talking with" rather than "talking at" each other. Term rather common in the field of religion; in other fields it may be called "open communication."

Feedback: Giving information to the person who originates any behavior about the consequences of that action or behavior. A common technique used in sensitivity training where members give feedback to other members about how they have been affected by their behavior. Similar to the "action-evaluation" idea used in relation to problem solving. Skill in feedback is quite difficult; too often becomes judgmental and hostile rather than simple, descriptive information.

Group Apathy: Condition in which group looks as if they weren't interested in what is going on. They may not be, but often because of unclear or confused purposes in the group, or lack of any agreed upon methods of working on the problem. Apathy or withdrawal are ways of handling frustration; often seen as a trait of the person when it actually may arise primarily from ineffective group procedures. Another way of handling frustration is through aggression and hostility; apathy or hostility may be symptoms of the same problems.

Group Cohesiveness: How well the group members will "stick together" because of their desire to be in the group; indicated by how much pressure, attack, shock, frustration, or whatever the group can take without breaking up. Often confused with harmony, or the avoidance of conflict or differences. Cohesive groups often show *more* conflict than other groups. People can differ without fear of losing their membership in the group, because of the supportive atmosphere. Usually a valuable condition in productivity.

Group Dynamics: Basically, the study of the processes and phenomena that occur in a small group; an area of social science, usually included under social psychology. Tends to give special attention to the "dynamic" or working processes and behavior in the group, hence is sometimes interpreted (incorrectly) to represent a particular way of working in groups; is sometimes used to allude to the laboratory or "sensitivity training" procedures.

Hidden Agenda: Purposes in the group which are not made explicit; may refer to purposes which a member has when he is trying to get the group to move in the direction he wants them to move without telling them; sometimes refers to purposes which the group may be trying to accomplish at an implicit or less conscious level. A group may be trying to make a work decision, but as it is doing that it may also be trying implicitly to keep certain members from talking too much.

Leadership Style: Particular way (role) a person who has been designated as leader attempts to handle his leadership responsibility; if done well, he will be most able to use his personality and his skills most effectively in a given situation. Not to be confused with democratic, autocratic or laissez-faire leadership which are arbitrary categories of behavior which often are used to assume that there is a "good" way to behave under all conditions, usually "democratic" behavior. Most important to have a leader develop a flexible style (sometimes democratic, sometimes autocratic, and sometimes laissez-faire) depending on the conditions and relationships within the group and the jobs to be done.

Role Playing: A training technique, used to help people understand interpersonal and group behavior; essentially asking a person to take some other pattern of behavior (role) other than his typical one, and to carry it out to see both how he reacts to it and how others react to him in the role. Used sometimes to illustrate working problems to groups, rather than talking about them. In general —represents the idea that people have many "roles" or patterns of behavior, and use different patterns in different situations. "Appropriate role" means doing the things in the group which are most helpful to the group.

Self-Oriented Behavior: Sometimes mis-interpreted as behavior which helps one maintain his "individuality"; actually, things which people do in order to satisfy themselves regardless of their effect on others or the group. Compare with "group-oriented" behavior, which are things people do which help the group get its work done and from which they can also get satisfaction.

Sensitivity Training: Frequently referred to as a T-Group (T for training, *not* for therapeutic); this kind of training gives major attention to the "process" of the group and attempts to help people improve their ability as a group to work together. It represents, in its design, a "process" oriented group in a rather pure form. It is a group which has as its purpose to help the members to improve their membership and interpersonal skills. It is not a group designed to do problem solving.

Supportive Atmosphere: Group situation in which members feel that they will not be personally judged or evaluated on the basis of their attempts to contribute to the group; one in which personal threat and rejection is minimal. Does not mean agreement; but it does mean that even though others in the group may differ with the ideas or suggestions expressed, they will not punish, degrade, or insult the contributor. Almost impossible to have a supportive atmosphere under conditions of competition; skills required are those of being able to disagree with a person without communicating any rejection. Not easy in our culture which tends to be judgmental. This atmosphere is required if members are to make their best contribution.

Task-Oriented vs Process-Oriented Groups: An artificial dichotomy; task orientation represents the condition when the group is working on some stated, explicit work problem (sometimes called "achievement problems"), something has to get done. Process orientation represents the condition when the group is trying to understand and improve its own working conditions (deal with "process problems"; improve communication or interpersonal relations). Process orientation differs from task orientation in that the job to be done is internal to the group, improving the skill of the group to work. It is really a different type of task, but still a task for the group.

CONCLUSION

So the wheel has come full circle. Our revels now are ended, and our wheels slow to a halt. We end where we began, with responding to God as true arbiter of our lives, not just our church days, our prayer hours, but our total lives: work, play, recreating, loving, praying, thinking, feeling, acting, deciding.

What does that have to do with team? Everything, as we have seen above. And in regard to teams opposing structural corruption, perhaps even more. For what society needs is to see again "how these Christians love one another."

I suggested above that teams operating on the values of the Gospel would probably spawn Christian communities: sharing of time, goods, energies, even houses. Witness the "parishes" of Holy Redeemer, Houston, and St. Patrick's, Providence, Rhode Island. Here community developed as members taking seriously the movement of the Spirit in their hearts began to *share*: goods, money, time, often feeding twenty-five to thirty people each day—and still surviving financially while they gave time to prayer and spread the Word freely, opening their hearts and homes to whoever wanted to come.[58]

Now, let's drop back to what this simple living-sharing pattern has to do with IBM, the Vatican, or the White House—you name the structure. Will they change because our team organization-skills, communications media, influential contacts, are all working at maximum? Some people do think so. I trust that Section VI (Team Technology) has proven that I DO believe in using *every* available tool, skill, and human resource.

But, then, we must end up saying: "We are unprofitable servants," and that's not a pain, but our security, our relaxation, our joy. For the triumph of the Spirit of Jesus, like Jesus' own victory while He was on earth, is not over the *exousiai* (powers of this world).[59] The place of the Spirit's primary victory is the human heart—where the trouble is. As habit-formers, we often become attached to persons, places, properties, and institutions, and so become their slaves because we fear either their loss or their power.

Clinton Morrison made the important distinction between the realm of Christ's authority (all things from the beginning) and the place of His victory (those who believe). Too often, we get lost complaining that the Church makes no difference to the powers of this world. True, to some extent, but what do we mean by "make a difference"?

When the early Christians surrendered their hearts to Christ and accepted His value-system (were born again), they came under the ever-growing influence of the Spirit and experienced a radical reorientation of their entire world.[60] Suddenly the "powers that be" lost power over them, and they were free to respond in the light of their deepest relationship: to Christ.

Made one with Him and incorporated into the Christian community, they experienced a new relationship to other people, structures, and society. Their problem was to keep that "new person," that new relationship with Christ, in the forefront of consciousness in every such relationship. Community became vital in this task, for God's love and forgiveness had to be *believed* to turn them into sources of strength to resist what went against Gospel-values and to do the serving it called for. If this faith failed, they again fell back into domination by the powers of this world, and Christ's work in them was fruitless (2 Cor. 6:1). Community helped and healed.

When we form teams for serving today, the same dynamic and process takes place:

(1) The change of heart that leads to the forgiveness of alienation, failure to grow and to love (Lk. 24:47), is God's free gift, longed for because of our experience of our own chipped-edges, our battle to become persons. This begins our deep-seated change. Then we press on trying to respond to love (*agape*), trying to widen and deepen the areas of change: religious, intellectual, moral, and emotional.[61]

(2) Then comes the move to share this joy, this striving, this prayer with others: the movement toward *community* (the team consolidates).

(3) Finally, the movement toward *social action*. Prayerful

study and sharing of Scripture, of worship, prayer, of communal goods, time, and energies awakens and enkindles the desire to serve. This sharing helps prove the reality of our growth and change. We go on through prayerful, communal discernment to choosing the field-white for serving according to the Spirit's direction.

It may well be a structure, for we are all embedded in them. Perhaps it will be an individual service, but no matter, we will be sharing and receiving gifts by serving, providing the ecology for the growth of our values, no matter what the area of service.

The choice is not a simplistic "choose to pray *or* to serve," nor is it figuring out the priority of degrees of corruption in various structures! Who we are: our unique gift of ourselves to the community, plus listening to the Spirit, plus what the community teaches us about ourselves—all these soon solve our questions about what field is ours for the serving. Listening to the Spirit through *prayer, events, people,* will call for the exercise of our gifts in *our* way, not imitating slavishly the style or the methods or the work of other team members. Only one question for all of us: have we surrendered the interior castle of our hearts to the Spirit so that we ARE people who try to make friends of all people, having gone down that road first ourselves? No, not in totality. That's the work of a lifetime, but are we working on that life-agenda of growing in love through the Spirit, of becoming persons, not through psychological tricks, but through a theological gift: the enabling power and love which is the Spirit embraced more nearly each day in our lives?

This makes the number one field-white for the harvest *our own hearts.* Far from being a program for hiding from social action, this following the call to four-fold personal conversion may even lead us deeper into the societal battle. If our gift is prophecy, in honesty we may be forced to speak out for God, often painfully, and with crucifying results in regard to our position, reputation, job, salary, and family, as once did Sir Thomas More upon the bank of Thames. Yet the same Spirit that impels us to speak shores us up with strength and joy, for as that same Londoner said once upon a time: "A man may lose his head and still come to no harm!"

When a team operates on these theological bases, joy and merriment in that same "More tradition" are the underlying thread of their "co-operation," for they have discovered the great secret of solving the greatest communication problem of all structures: the human difference of individual See-Levels.

Since each individual person's gifts are a message from the Spirit, they are to be respected, not resented; to be cherished, not suppressed. Difference is beautiful, says the Spirit. Surely, God must be messy, She so loves variety. Can we, as team, cherish it too? On that answer, perhaps, hangs the fate of our mission.

All things counter, original, spare, strange;
Whatever is fickle, freckled (who knows how?)
With swift, slow; sweet, sour; adazzle, dim;
He fathers-forth whose beauty is past change:
        PRAISE HIM!

        Gerard M. Hopkins, SJ, "Pied Beauty"

NOTES

1. See Andrew Greeley's *Building Coalitions* (Franklin Watts) for the use of coalitions in political action.

2. Bernard Lonergan, *Insight, A Study in Human Understanding* (New York: 1965), p. 65.

3. *Loc. cit.*

4. "She" in reference to the Holy Spirit will be used throughout this text not because God is feminine, but because we can no longer think of God as solely masculine (also an inadequate concept). Because my goal is to encourage the participation of the laity and especially of women on teams, I choose to use the feminine appellation for the Holy Spirit and with some good historical precedent. One among many: the Didascalia 2.26.5-6; the woman deacon symbolized the Holy Spirit in the primitive Church of the time: "Diaconissa vero in typum sancti spiritus honoretur a vobis." My usage neither disparages nor ignores men's roles on teams but rather strengthens a sharing by women on teams historically suppressed and very weak today in the Christian churches, yet a sharing vitally needed for total ministry.

5. Jean LaCroix, in Garaudy's *Perspectives de L'Homme* (Paris: Presses Universitaires, 1961).

6. Gregory of Nyssa, *Life of Moses*, pg. 44.404A-D. See the English text of H. Musurillo, SJ, in *Glory to Glory* (New York: Chas. Scribner's Sons, 1961).

7. Hugh O'Neill, SJ, "The Concept of Value," unpublished paper.

8. Teilhard de Chardin, SJ, *The Divine Milieu* (New York: 1960), p. 41.

9. St. Benedict's team is made up of Sr. Toinette Eugene PBVM, Rev. James Keeley, Sr. Sharon Flanagan, SHF., and Rev. Paul Vassar.

10. William S. Clebsch and Charles R. Jaekle, *Pastoral Care in Historical Perspective* (New York: Harper and Row, 1967), p. 4.

11. Philip Murnion, "Understanding Pastoral Ministry," *Catholic Mind*, February 1974, pp. 41-47.

12. *Ibid.*, p. 45.

13. Report of the Subcommittee on the Systematic Theology of Priesthood of the National Council of Catholic Bishops' Committee on Priestly Life and Ministry, p. 24.

14. Donald Gelpi, SJ, "Conscience," *Experiencing God*, soon to be published by Paulist Press.

15. Donald Gelpi, SJ, "The Gifts," *Charism and Sacrament*, (New York: Paulist Press, 1976).

16. See in this connection ("disappearing" as essential to ministry)

Michel de Certeau's fine article, "How is Christianity Thinkable Today," *Theology Digest*, Winter 1972, p. 341.

17. John McCall, "Conversion," humorous and penetrating analysis of the psychological process of change of heart. (NCR Cassette: Kansas City, Mo.)

18. René Laurentin, "Editorial," *The New Concilium*, Vol. 80, (New York: Herder & Herder, 1972), p. 9.

19. *Ibid.*, pp. 14-15.

20. Gelpi, *Charism and Sacrament, op. cit.*

21. *Loc. cit.*

22. *Loc. cit.*

23. *One Baptism One Eucharist and a Mutually Recognized Ministry* (Three Agreed Statements), Faith and Order Paper #73, World Council of Churches, Geneva, Switzerland, p. 45.

24. Robert F. Mager, *Goal Analysis* (Belmont, Calif.: Fearon Publishers, 1972), p. 23. Highly recommended for goal-setting, attitudes, and goal-analysis; a book a team might work through together.

25. Training Enterprises—New Techniques, Inc. of Seattle, Wash., P.O. Box 1941, produces an entire series of Team Building Tools: Norms, Skills, Group Interaction, etc.

26. In this connection, a collection like *Women and Orders*, edited by Robert Heyer of Paulist Press, gives women-servers a look at a wide spectrum of stimulating ideas to meditate upon and build self-concept, breaking down stereotypes and opening up thinking to the leading of the Spirit when it comes time to decide about gifts and roles.

27. Letty Russell, Th.D., "Theological Aspects of the Partnership of Women and Men in Christian Communities," paper given at Louvain Colloquium, 1975, p. 9.

28. Paul K. Jewett. *Man as Male and Female: A Study in Sexual Relationships from a Theological Point of View* (New York: Eerdmans), p. 14.

29. Louis Evely. *That Man is You.*

30. The Johari Window, designed by Joseph Luft and Harry Ingham.

31. See Reuel L. Howe's *Miracle of Dialogue* (Connecticut, 1963) for further work on communication.

32. For a fine study of change theory, see Dorwin Cartwright, *Achieving Change in People: Some Applications of Group Dynamics Theory*, Leadership Laboratory Reading, University of California, Berkeley, California.

33. For a penetrating look at the Christian's relationship to the structures (powers) of this world, see Clinton E. Morrison, *The Powers That Be* (London: SCM Press, 1960). A view treated specifically in the section on social evil (Chapter VII).

34. Chris Argyris, "Research Trends in Executive Behavior," *Leadership in Action* (Washington, D.C.: 1961), p. 16.

35. Christopher Dawson, *The Historic Reality of Christian Culture* (New York: 1960), p. 27.

36. This description of team-member roles is taken from Kenneth Benne and Paul Sheats, "Functional Roles of Group Members," *Group Development*, 1960.

37. Paulo Freire's *Pedagogy of the Oppressed* (New York: Herder & Herder, 1972) is an analysis of getting the circular model into institutional form, giving responsibility to those who must carry out the action. Adding the faith and fire of the Charismatic Movement to Freire's methodology would make a fine blend for teams to try out as agents of social change.

38. Recommended for ideas on this: Stephen Clark, *Building Christian Community* (Notre Dame: Ave Maria Press, 1972). See also: Louis A. Hoffart, OMI. *Charismatic Transformation of the Parish: A Rationale and a Model for Parish Renewal*, M.A. Thesis, Jesuit School of Theology, Berkeley, 1975. Steve Clark's *Unordained Elders and Renewal Communities* (New York: Paulist Press, 1976) notes that the patristic period of Christian history gives us the precedent of ordaining the leader(s) of such renewal communities to the presbyterate (priesthood) as a means of integrating such communities into the existing structure of the church at the time.

39. See Sr. Maria Augusta Neal, *Social Encyclicals: Role of Women*, presented at the Bishops' Bicentennial hearings in Washington, D.C., February 3, 1975: most useful for the role of patriarchy in perpetuating conformism and unquestioning followership.

40. Martin Heidegger, "Hölderlin and the Essence of Poetry," *Existence and Being*, p. 31.

41. Craig Haney and Philip Zimbardo, "It's Tough to Tell a High School from a Prison," *Psychology Today*, June 1975, p. 26.

42. Duncan Neuhauser, "The Hospital as Matrix Organization," *Hospital Administration*, Fall 1972. Dr. Neuhauser explains Contingency Theory highlighting the role of teams, especially the importance of the patient-care team for lateral coordination and the need for good team-management. He sees the role of the attending physician, specifying in detail the tasks of other team members, as an inappropriate technique to the extent that these other team members are also truly professionalized.

43. Stephan Pfürtner, "Pathology of the Catholic Church," *Ongoing Reform of the Church, Concilium*, Vol. 73 (Pastoral) ed. Alois Muller and Norbert Greinacher (New York: Herder and Herder, 1972), p. 30.

44. Laurentin, *op. cit.* This entire volume needs careful reading, especially of the significant parallels between the New Testament and our own period.

45. Pfürtner, *op. cit.*, p. 33.

46. Part of reform (conversion) of the Church-as-Healer will be an acceptance of the totality of human experience. Donald Gelpi, SJ, in *Charism and Sacrament*, presents a method of doing theology that includes the aspect of *feeling*, making it basic to his treatment of gifts, sac-

raments, and Trinity, a very liberating experience, and one which helps to lead to the sharing mentioned on p. 00.

47. Albert Outler, "Church: 'Mission Field,' " *National Catholic Reporter*, 13, December 1974.

48. Laurentin, *op. cit.* p. 11. See also Raymond E. Brown's fine treatment of the biblical basis for both offices in his *Priest and Bishop* (New York: Paulist Press, 1970).

49. John T. Pawlikowski, "The Minister as Pharisee," *Commonweal*, 21 January 1972.

50. Mark O. Hatfield, "An Economics for Sustaining Humanity," *Post American*, Vol. 4.3.19, March 1975.

51. *Ibid.*

52. Here Hatfield is quoting Claude Levi-Strauss.

53. Teams interested in prison ministry could begin by studying *Struggle for Justice: A Report of Crime and Punishment in America*, prepared by the American Friends Service Committee (New York: Hill and Wang, 1971), usually obtained from their local office. I hope to publish in 1978 a booklet on prison ministry entitled *Jacket* to treat this area separately, given the magnitude of the problem.

54. Louis J. Putz, CSC, "Not by Bread Alone," *Connector*, No. 5, February 1975, ed. John J. Egan, CCUM, Notre Dame, Indiana.

55. The Alliance for Displaced Homemakers operates out of 4223 Telegraph Avenue, Oakland, Calif. 9470. Tish Sommers has published a helpful book, *The Not So Helpless Female* (New York: David McKay Company, 1973), pushing the idea of women working together in teams. She sets forth easy ways to organize people for action and to effect change, especially how women have done and can do this. Especially good for how to build coalitions.

56. Clarence and Edith Roberts of Martinez, California are responsible for 15 centers (Oakland, California) out of which *Sharing of Scriptures* groups operate. Their booklet will appear soon. Their series of lessons appears in *Catholic Charismatic* magazine.

57. Laurentin, *op. cit.* p. 16.

58. Louis Hoffart, OMI, describes this parish in his thesis, which also contains a fine bibliography.

59. Morrison, *op. cit.* p. 124.

60. *Ibid.*, 125.

61. Donald Gelpi, SJ. *Charism and Sacrament op. cit.* 1.18. describes this four-fold conversion as (1) *religious:* assuming personal responsibility for responding in an appropriate manner to every impulse of divine grace; (2) *affective:* balanced emotional growth; (3) *intellectual:* responsibility for false and inadequate beliefs, and (4) *moral:* responsibility for acting out the demands of one's enlightened beliefs.

BIBLIOGRAPHY

Anderson, Martin. *Multiple Ministries: Staffing the Local Church.* Minneapolis, Minn., Augsburg Publishing House.

Barlow, T. Edward. *Small Group Ministry in the Contemporary Church.* Independence, Missouri, Herald Publishing House, 1972.

Brewer, Earl D.C. *Protestant Parish.* Atlanta, Comm. Arts Press, 1967.

Cartwright, Dorin. *Achieving Change in People.* Berkeley, University of California, Leadership Laboratory Reading.

Clark, Stephen. *Building Christian Community.* Notre Dame, Indiana, Ave Maria Press, 1972.

———. *Unordained Elders and Renewal Communities.* New York, Paulist Press, 1976).

Clebsch, William A. and Charles R. Jaekle. *Pastoral Care in Historical Perspective.* New York, Harper & Row, 1967.

Clinebell, H.J. *The Mental Health of the Local Church.* Nashville, Tenn., Abingdon Press, 1972.

Cooney, Sr. Caritas. "Pastoral Team Ministry." *Connector,* Vol. 2, No. 1, October 1975.

Corazzini, John. "Team Ministry." *Catholic World,* January 1971.

Curran, Charles E. *The Crisis in Priestly Ministry.* Notre Dame, Indiana, Fides Press, 1972.

Egan, Gerard. *Face to Face.* Monterey, California, Brooks-Cole Company, 1973.

Fukuyama, Yoshio. *The Ministry in Transition.* University Park, Pennsylvania, Pennsylvania State University Press, 1973.

Futrell, John C. *Making an Apostolic Community of Love.* St. Louis, Missouri, Institute of Jesuit Resources Seminar, 1970.

Gelpi, Donald. *Charism and Sacrament.* New York, Paulist Press, 1976.

———. *Experiencing God* (unpublished manuscript).

Guerrette, Richard H. *A New Identity for the Priest.* New York, Paulist Press, 1973.

Goldbruner, Josef. *Realization (The Anthropology of Pastoral Care).* Notre Dame, Indiana, Notre Dame Univ. Press, 1966.

Glasse, James D. *Profession: Minister.* New York, Abingdon, 1968.

Greeley, Andrew. *Priests in the United States: Reflections on a Survey.* New York, Doubleday, 1972.

Hall, Douglas T. and Benjamin Schneider. *Organizational Climates and Careers: The Work Lives of Priests.* New York, Seminar Press, 1973.

Heyer, Robert. *Women and Orders.* New York, Paulist Press, 1975.

Judy, Marvin T. *The Multiple Staff Ministry.* Nashville, Abingdon Press, 1970.

Jud, Gerald J., et al. *Ex-Factors: Why Men Leave the Parish Ministry.* Philadelphia, Pilgrim Press, 1970.

Kelly, Frank, "Reflections on Building a Community of Faith." *Connector.* Vol. 2, No. 3, December 1975.

Kerans, Patrick. *Sinful Social Structures.* New York, Paulist Press, 1975.

Lange, Joseph and Anthony Cushing. *Worshipping Community.* New York, Paulist Press, 1976.

Lakein, Alan. *How to Get Control of Your Time and Your Life.* New York, P. Wyden, Inc., 1973.

Larkin, Ernest E. *Spiritual Renewal of the American Priesthood.* Washington, D.C., U.S. Catholic Conference Publications, 1972.

Lewis, G. Douglass, ed. *Explorations in Ministry.* New York, IDOC, North America, 1971.

Mager, Robert. *Goal Analysis.* Belmont, California, Fearon Publishers, 1972.

Maslow, A.H. "Self-Actualizing People," *Personality Symposium.* New York, Grune & Stratton, 1950.

Mitchell, K. *Psychological and Theological Relationship in Multiple Staff Ministry.* Philadelphia, Westminster, 1966.

Nouwen, Henri. *The Wounded Healer.* New York, Doubleday, 1972.

Putz, Louis. "Not By Bread, Alone," *Connector*, No. 5, February 1975.

Rahner, Karl. *Theology of Pastoral Action.* New York, Herder & Herder, 1968.

Stogdill, Ralph. *Handbook of Leadership.* New York, The Free Press, 1974.

Swidler, Leonard, and Arlene Swidler, eds. *Bishops and People*, a collection of articles by members of the Catholic Theological Faculty of Tubingen. Philadelphia, Westminster Press, 1970.

Team Ministry. An Occasional Paper. London, Westminster, The Methodist Church Home Department, April 1972.

"Team Ministry Guidelines." Division of Theological Education, The American Lutheran Church, 422 S. Fifth St., Minneapolis, Minnesota.

"Team Ministry/the Hartford Model," a summary of the study conducted by CARA (Center for Applied Research in the Apostolate), *Origins*, Vol. 5, No. 13, 18 September 1975.

von Campenhausen, Hans. *Tradition and Life in the Church.* Philadelphia, Fortress Press, 1960.